Jenny Herbert has been part of the tourism industry for more than twenty years, and has frequently travelled to Europe. In this book she uses her experience on both sides of tourism to give practical advice and insider information, and to share some of her special travelling experiences.

THE INTELLIGENT TRAVELLER
How to plan your perfect trip

JENNY HERBERT

The Five Mile Press

The Five Mile Press Pty Ltd
1 Centre Road, Scoresby
Victoria 3179 Australia
Email: publishing@fivemile.com.au
Website: www.fivemile.com.au

Copyright © Jenny Herbert, 2008

All rights reserved. No part of this book may be
reproduced, stored in a retrieval system, or transmitted
by any form or by any means, electronic, mechanical,
photocopying, recording or otherwise, without the
prior written permission of the publisher.

First published 2008
Reprinted 2008

Printed in China

Edited by Brooke Clark
Cover design by Blue Cork
Illustrations by Gaston Vanzet
Page design by Zoë Murphy

National Library of Australia Cataloguing-in-Publication data
Herbert, Jenny.
The intelligent traveller : how to plan your perfect
holiday.

1st ed.

Bibliography.

ISBN 978 1 74178 646 0 (pbk.).

1. Travel - Planning. I. Title.

910

ACKNOWLEDGEMENTS

Thank you, my dear family and friends, for your suggestions, valuable criticisms and careful reading: Joan Fail, Peter LeRoy, Jenny Fraser-Smith, Hendrik Forster and Andrea Fail. Thanks Simon Hills at Icon Holidays, Geoffrey Conaghan and Steve Palombo at Melbourne Airport, and Andrew Marshall at Qantas for valuable industry information. Mostly, thanks to Fred – my strongest supporter, and my life's travelling companion.

CONTENTS

PREFACE ... ix

1 WAY TO GO ... 1

2 GETTING STARTED ... 17

3 AIR AND GROUND: GETTING AROUND ... 43

4 HOMES AWAY FROM HOME ... 77

5 MONEY MATTERS ... 101

6 WHAT AND HOW TO PACK ... 115

7 THE REAL THING ... 129

8 ON THE MOVE ... 151

9 FOOD, HEALTH AND FITNESS ... 167

10 JOURNEY'S END ... 197

READING GUIDE ... 204

PLEASE NOTE

The websites referred to in this book offer a wealth of information. However, this book does not endorse the sites beyond the suggestion that they may help you with your travel plans.

*You are welcome to photocopy the spreadsheets and checklists for your own use. They can also be found on The Five Mile Press's website **www.fivemile.com.au** for you to print out and use.*

PREFACE

Twenty years from now you will be more disappointed by the things that you didn't do than by the ones you did do. So throw off the bowlines. Sail away from the safe harbor. Catch the trade winds in your sails. Explore. Dream. Discover.

Mark Twain

Around 450 BCE Herodotus set out to explore beyond his homeland Greece. With native curiosity he travelled to understand how others lived: their religions, customs and techniques. He returned with stories of wonder, mystery and humour. He was, perhaps, the first tourist. Travel spread to a wider population as pilgrims went in search of religious certainty and healing. The Romans' skills in road building opened the known world to more and more people who journeyed for trade, ritual and military exploits. With sailing ships was born a passion for exploration, and sailors brought home tales of strange, exotic places. Tourism's fortunes waxed and waned over the centuries, but by the time the steam engine introduced reliability and economy to travel, movement, like agriculture, had become an unquestioned human activity.

Travelling is recreation in its truest sense: re-creation, because rarely can you return home unchanged by your experience. Once it gets under your skin, it becomes a passion to be indulged whenever time and fortune allows. But where to start? It's a big world out there, and there are complexities to be mastered and tasks to be completed to ensure your travels reward you with both pleasure and enlightenment.

Having decided to travel, this book will help you to make the most of your experience. It is designed primarily for those undertaking long-haul travel, especially from Australia to Europe, but many of the principles apply even if you're only driving a couple of hours from home to your favourite beachside town.

There are plenty of books on the market about the world's destinations; this is a resource to complement your guidebooks. It will help you with all the matters that don't traditionally come within the scope of guidebooks: how to anticipate, plan, research, budget and enjoy whatever destination you choose.

Like travel itself, this book ranges from the pragmatic to the eclectic. Some of the chapters focus on the practicalities that are important to help your travels flow seamlessly: passports and budgeting, packing and keeping safe. Others take a more philosophical tack towards the abstract elements of open minds and fresh eyes, to ponder the worth and need for curiosity, independent observation and sense of purpose. Both angles are essential for a truly fulfilling trip.

Chapter 1 will set you on the path to your holiday. No matter what your motivation to travel, to achieve your goals you need to put in the hard yards of planning.

For a young backpacker the thought of jumping on a plane and letting events take their course might sound exciting, but for most travellers, holiday time is limited and precious, and we need to minimise the risk of it being spoilt. The more you know in advance, the more smoothly your holiday will run, and the more receptive you'll be to the new world unfolding around you.

Planning reduces stress. If you've already worked out what to expect, what you can afford to spend, where you will stay and so on, you're then free to open yourself to unexpected moments of serendipity. These special experiences will pass you by if you're scrambling for accommodation, or trying to work out why the ATM won't give you money.

The chapter also considers the importance of anticipation. It's a pleasure so often neglected, or rejected as unimportant, yet it can stretch your holiday time as in preparation you seek out a special place to stay, or lose yourself in a book about the history of the country you're going to.

So many people rush to get away: they work up to the last moment, push clothes into a suitcase and drop into their aircraft seat exhausted. Throughout the flight, their minds churn over what they've forgotten to do or pack, or they worry about what to expect at the end of the flight. This not only makes travel more exhausting, it also means you lose a couple of days at the start of your holiday while you recover. What a waste. Chapter 2 covers the practical tasks that you must undertake in the early part of your planning, including passports, visas and insurance. Get these out of the way early and you'll then be ready to explore the absorbing tasks of choosing accommodation and forms of travel. This chapter also helps you to set up systems to manage all the information you will collect as you move through the planning process. The checklists in this book, starting in Chapter 2, will help to relieve the stress inherent in rushing, even if you can't get around the last-minute pressures of your job.

Also in this chapter, we start to consider that travel comes at a price both to the environment and to local populations. We can no longer ignore the fact that flying is a significant contributor of greenhouse gas emissions. And in many of the key destinations around the world, local people are drowning beneath the tide of mass tourism, many without reaping any of the economic benefits. So we need to adopt a responsible approach to our travels, to reduce our impact on the environment and avoid undermining the very things we have gone to see. There are travel tips throughout the book on being alert and sensitive to these issues.

Chapter 3 sets things in motion with advice about long-haul flights – everything from how to enjoy an in-flight meal, deal with a problem passenger and survive the dreariness of in-transit stops, to the best ways to approach booking this expensive part of your travels. From here the chapter moves on to consider the broad range of transport options available during your holiday: trains and ferries, motorhomes and hire cars. You can start to be adventurous, the less usual methods of travel can offer the best holiday highlights.

In Chapter 4, we look at the huge choice of accommodation options, and especially how to find something special using the internet. The internet has changed the nature of travel research, giving independent travellers a fantastic tool to investigate beyond the obvious. On the other side of the equation, the internet has given small tourism businesses the opportunity to take their products to the world. If you are web-savvy, the range of choice is prodigious and easily accessible.

You'll see that I have a strong preference for self-contained accommodation as it's a way of finding something more representative of the local lifestyle, and also helps to protect the budget from the high cost, in most places, of regularly dining out.

To many people, the main decision to make about their overseas holiday is where to go. Having made that decision, they hand over the planning to a travel agent. While travel agents certainly have their place, they make their money on volume, that is, mass-market travel choices, and rarely have access to the tiny, out of the way, delightfully different aspects of a destination that can make travel so beguiling. The travel industry is focused mainly on the prominent and the easy to book – large hotel chains and tour companies that are stereotypical throughout the world. This book is for those who want to build their journey around niche accommodation options that are unusual and more in tune with the local culture and environment.

Big business, by its nature, practises a sort of arm's length, sanitised approach to hospitality, whereas small businesses offer an opportunity for you to get close to a local. The owners of small businesses are the people who can take you 'under the skin' of a destination, and are more likely to treat you as a guest rather than a customer. If you ask, they'll tell you about what really matters to them, what they love about where they live, and what special features of their location you must not miss. Their intimate knowledge – and pride – is part of the unique experience you are buying when you choose them.

Underpinning your holiday enjoyment will be the security of knowing that you can afford what you're doing. In Chapter 5, we look at holiday budgeting along with other money matters such as traveller's cheques, tips for using credit cards, ways to manage receipts and how to claim tax refunds. There's even a brief consideration of the etiquette of tipping.

Then it's on to the art of packing. In Chapter 6 you can discover ways of travelling light and easy, the extras you'll need to consider, and what's allowed on airlines. There are tips about types of clothing, size of suitcases, style of walking shoes and the benefits of a backpack. There are 'wash and go' ideas, and there's advice on how to dress comfortably for a long flight.

Along with all the material items to pack, it's also important to pack some purpose into your travels. Chapter 7 moves away from the practical to consider the rewards of thoughtfulness and curiosity. There's more to travel than seeing the sights. There are untold opportunities for inquiry and transformation, provided you are willing to open your eyes to the wonders, and open your mind to the world's kaleidoscope.

In Chapter 8 we return to more practical considerations that will aid you while you're on the move. This chapter looks at strategies for being a good travel companion, finding your way around and keeping safe, and tells you what to do if things go wrong. There are some ideas on how to move beyond the pull of shopping, and where to find places in big cities to take a break from sightseeing.

Chapter 9 encompasses two sides of the one travel coin: enjoying good food and avoiding putting on weight. Food is an integral part of the travel experience – the more unfamiliar the food, the more you appreciate how far you are from home. The food section celebrates culinary difference, and helps you immerse yourself in the heady food aromas of foreign shores. There are suggestions on what and where to eat, as well as tips for market shopping and buying local produce.

The section on fitness is a guide to staying mobile and flexible throughout your travels, from enduring the cramped quarters of a plane to avoiding the museum shuffle. The advice starts with health and fitness preparation, and moves on to exercises that are arranged by holiday activity, and there's a good argument for walking to save your waistline and the environment.

All good things come to an end, but the advantage of travel is that the memories stay for a lifetime. The final chapter looks at what you might bring home to help you shore up memories, and how to allow the experience of your travels to add depth and colour to your everyday life.

So now it's time to fasten your seatbelt, stow your tray table, put your seat in the upright position, and get set for take-off. I hope you enjoy your travels.

1

WAY TO GO

Travel is more than seeing the sights; it is a change that goes on, deep and permanent, in the ideas of living.

Miriam Beard

- Why travel?
- Where in the world will you go?
- Take time to plan
- Language and difference
- Choosing a focus
- When to go
- Gathering information
- Reading as preparation
- Building anticipation

WHY TRAVEL?

You start to toss around the possibility of travelling overseas. At first, the idea comes upon you slowly, then excitement builds. Dates are considered, destinations researched, budgets calculated. It all looks possible; it's time to turn a dream into reality, time to say the magic words: *let's go*.

But why do we bother to travel? Why go to the effort, the discomfort and the expense that's involved in leaving home for unknown shores, when we could curl up in front of the fire with a ripping yarn of faraway places and exotic cultures?

At any one time, it's estimated that there are between 3 and 5 million people flying across the sky. Europe absorbs 220 million visitors a year – Venice alone has 20 million visitors each year. Just think of all those people moving about the world, the teeming crowds at train stations, the jostling hordes at major attractions, the milling mobs at airports. It's a wonder we even contemplate joining this ever-rising tide of tourists.

Yet we do contemplate travel, and come to the conclusion that despite the drawbacks, it is too wonderful an experience to miss. Why?

We travel for the sheer pleasure, but also to find something that matters deeply, to discover more about ourselves, to make life more meaningful, and to better understand the world. Of course, this is not a universal intention, as is glaringly obvious when watching the crowds at Manchester airport waiting for their cheap flights to Estonia, where they go for the cheap beer and to behave badly in someone else's backyard. At the other extreme are travellers who seek something sacred, such as those who follow in the footsteps of the fourteenth-century pilgrims who made their way to Santiago de Compostela equipped only with a small satchel and a walking stick. Yet even pilgrims can't avoid the modern-day realities of passport queues and jetlag.

Travelling allows us to 'get away from it all', but it also gives us an opportunity to view our life through a different prism. It's not to have our beliefs and prejudices confirmed, but to open us up to strangeness. This is almost impossible to achieve at home, where habitual behaviour stifles any attempt to look at the world afresh. Routine begets routine, familiarity begets familiarity – home is no place to search for new horizons.

If you travel to seek intrinsic meaning and personal value in a holiday, you need to move beyond unimaginative, unthinking packaging to find a point where difference challenges and history informs.

For pilgrims, meaning and purpose are synonymous with religious and sacred experiences, but the sacred nature of their quests is not for everyone. Travel can have purpose even if it doesn't have piety. We can stand in awe of the flying buttresses soaring of a Norman cathedral, or the emotional integrity of a work of art, or the simple modesty of a traditional song, provided we have the right state of mind.

It's a state of mind for looking beyond the obvious – pulling back the veil of tourism – that matters. It's taking your fingernail to the surface experience and scratching away the veneer to reveal the authenticity beneath. Yet many travellers fail to even register the veneer. They chatter their way through one country after another, clicking away the images to possess what they have not felt, and return home with a sense of conquest rather than fulfilment. It's an experience that finds more parallel in the purchase of a new toaster than the achievement of a personal goal.

Once, in the Piazza del Campo in Sienna, a tourist was raging that the shops had closed during the afternoon. 'Don't they know they're missing out on my money,' she fumed. That the siesta is one of the foundations of the culture she had come to experience was lost to her. That the Italians would value their siesta more than her few American dollars seemed, to her, pure madness.

A friend of mine tells an amusing anecdote about Peter Hilary that illustrates the gulf between different travel motivations. Hilary was in Kathmandu preparing to climb Mount Everest. He and his party were surrounded by sophisticated climbing and camping gear as they made their final checks. A woman in high heels and swathes of gold jewellery stopped to ask Hilary where he was going. 'Mount Everest,' he replied. 'Oh, you'll love it,' she gushed, 'we did it yesterday.'

But what's *your* motivation for travelling? The answer to this question will determine the sort of holiday you take, how you plan, how you travel and where you go. Is this to be your once-in-a-lifetime splurge, or one of many trips you plan to make?

Everyone has their personal reasons for travelling: from seeking knowledge to shopping, from visiting friends and relatives to witnessing a moment in history. You might travel to be awed by nature or spectacular architecture, or to seek a place where you can truly slow down and relax. But behind the reasons, for the thoughtful traveller there is a desire to be taken outside the everyday world, to be challenged by difference. Otherwise, why go to the expense and effort of overseas travel, if a drink around the pool is all you really need? Once you set your sights on a foreign country, exploring the foreignness becomes the purpose.

WHERE IN THE WORLD WILL YOU GO?

For me, anticipation always starts with getting out the atlas. I love poring over the countries, tracing the outline of their borders with my finger, mouthing the unfamiliar names of towns and rivers, working out distances and geographical features. Travel allows you to discover the wealth of colour and culture across the globe. As you become familiar with one country after another, you come to understand where their histories overlap, how they interact, in what ways they remain unique, the shape of their coastlines, the length of their mountain ranges, their place in a globalised world.

> **WEB SEARCH**
> Google Earth http://earth.google.com is good for a bird's-eye view of plains, mountains, rivers and coastlines

As you travel more and more, a second layer of knowledge forms over this crust: how a country's history has unfolded, its culture and food, what sort of people make up the population. Such unfolding knowledge is, for me, the wonder and joy of travelling.

If this is your first overseas foray, you'll want to visit the major sights (Buckingham Palace, the Eiffel Tower, the Parthenon etc) – not only because they are spectacular and important and you've heard about them all your life, but also because they can provide the starting point for discovering the world. They are usually iconic because of their importance – to architecture, to history, to the natural environment – and therefore there is a mass of information for you to easily access.

TRAVEL TIP
Ask yourself, truthfully: 'How much can I absorb and understand in one day, or one week?'

WEB SEARCH
Some sites for research:
- SBS produces the definitive *World Guide*, which you can purchase through their website www20.sbs.com.au/worldguide
- www.dfat.gov.au/geo is the part of the Department of Foreign Affairs and Trade website that includes detailed information on foreign countries: land, people, government, economy, political conditions etc
- www.cia.gov/library/publications/the-world-factbook is full of facts about countries.
  The information is as dry as sticks but you might find something of interest
- www.tripadvisor.com for information and reviews about accommodation (but it's very subjective)
- www.europeforvisitors.com for general information such as transport, tourist offices and maps
- www.visiteurope.com is the website of the 36 member countries of the European Travel Commission
- www.unesco.org for World Heritage sites

Even if this is your first major overseas trip, try to avoid the trap of too many places or countries in too few weeks. Every time you change country you can expect to lose a day to travelling; too many changes means too many days lost. And you need at least a few days in any one place to start to absorb its character (rather than the 'it's Tuesday so this must be Barcelona' syndrome). So write your wish list, then use the travel tips below to see if it is practicable within your time frame. Start to cull, depending on what you are seeking from your holiday.

TRAVEL TIP
Your initial planning needs to include the following:
- the number of days you'll be away
- your departure and return dates
- the countries you want to visit, and why
- the number of nights at each location

- the sites you want to visit at each location (have you allowed sufficient time?)
- the distances and ease of travel between locations
- the possible forms of travel: air, train, coach, hire car

In your early stages of planning, be sure to build in opportunities for slow time: it is the kernel of special moments. It might be strolling along streets for no purpose other than to look at houses or shops, dawdling over coffee while you watch the locals going about their lives, enjoying a picnic in a famous garden on a sunny afternoon, or (my favourite) shopping at the food markets, rubbing shoulders with the locals.

TAKE TIME TO PLAN

Whether it's the selection of a good pair of walking shoes, or studying maps to work out the highways you'll travel, planning is as fundamentally important to successful travel as it is to successful business.

It takes time – a lot of time if you're going to get it right – but it will pay huge dividends as you move around the world, knowing what to expect, how to find your accommodation, what time the next train leaves, and so much more. It's also fun, and it builds anticipation.

Travel is no different from any other of life's projects – you will get from it what you put in. Research, learning, planning, exploring: these are the preliminary steps that will set you on a path towards a holiday with depth, personal value and special memories. This preliminary work – the planning and the dreaming – is part of the travel experience. The period of anticipation will extend your holiday beyond just the time you spend away.

Planning an overseas trip can take remarkably little effort if you don't want to immerse yourself in the process. You can decide on a few well-known destinations, choose your dates, and hand everything over to a travel agent to arrange. There's nothing wrong with this, but it won't ever allow you to delve beneath the obvious, to seek the special out-of-the-way place that will make your travel experience zing.

There's more to know before you go than the times of your flights and the addresses of your hotels. Being pre-armed with a whole range of information will significantly reduce the stress of the unfamiliar while increasing the enjoyment. Maps are wonderful for this – street maps, airport maps, railway and highway route maps – all these build layer upon layer of knowledge that will help you to confidently embrace a totally foreign country.

LANGUAGE AND DIFFERENCE

For English speakers, travel is made easy because at so many destinations the language is understood, and often spoken fluently as a second language. This is a great help if you are trying to explain a problem to a pharmacist, or a dietary need at a restaurant, but it does take some of the special shine from the experience of travel. If we go seeking difference, to have our own way of life and beliefs challenged, then we need to step outside our comfort zone.

On the other hand, travelling to another country where English is the first language can be disorienting in its own way. Because the language is the same, we expect other things will be the same, so the subtle differences are more difficult to pinpoint. Rather, we're left with an uneasiness of not quite understanding, but not knowing why. On my first trip to London, I expected to find it very similar to home – the country of my forebears and of Australia's heritage should hold no real surprises. But even from the air, before landing at Heathrow, the rows and rows of identical terrace houses were a tangible and startling indication of the degree of historical and social divergence.

It is sometimes easier to learn more about a country where English is not the first language. We anticipate difference, expect that we will be challenged and willingly go looking for expressions of other ways of life. It can be frustrating when you meet someone who you suspect has really interesting stories to tell, but without a common language, you can't have a meaningful conversation, and so miss out on valuable personal insights. However, a ready willingness to try to understand seems to overcome many language barriers.

In Agrigento, we* strolled along the Corso, past the sentries in their bullet-proof boxes with their automatic rifles (evidence of Mafiosi everywhere). At a souvenir shop we stopped to buy a Jew's Harp. The shopkeeper held the small instrument against his teeth and plucked the strings. His wife grasped my arm. '*Scacciapensieri*,' she tried to make us understand but we didn't know the word. Through a gentle pantomime of signs and sighs she acted out the feelings of longing and nostalgia and helped us to understand that this was the music of their history. Such universal expression doesn't need a shared language.

Sometimes, it's the other way around. Dining in Munich, I asked if instead of meat, could I please have just a salad? The waiter clearly understood my language; it was my dietary preference that the stout Bavarian found incomprehensible.

Nonetheless, some form of dictionary is essential, even if just for emergencies. If you're technologically committed you can buy devices that give voice translations for any number of everyday words. But my preference is for Robert Dessaix's advice (in his essay *Do You Speak English?*) of using a piece of cardboard on which you've written the most likely words you'll need, folded and carried in your pocket.

> **WEB SEARCH**
> http://australia.ectaco.com
> for electronic language translation devices

CHOOSING A FOCUS

Understanding your motivation for travel will have a bearing on your choice of destinations. But it's always good to travel with a purpose, a special interest that helps give focus to your travels so they don't become aimless wanders from one major attraction to another, or worse, one hotel room to another, with little understanding and no insight.

---

* 'We' throughout this book refers to me and my husband Fred.

You might start with the purpose of travelling to the cradle of civilisation, or exploring the connections of nautical history between England and Portugal. You might want to study the lace-making techniques in Brugge and Burano, or the pottery of Limoges in France and Portmeirion in Wales. You could set a challenge of taking every possible steam train trip in Britain, or travelling the breadth of Germany on riverboats and barges. You could choose to immerse yourself in the music of a country, or its cuisine. You could follow the footsteps of Stephen Dedalus through Dublin, or of Mrs Dalloway through London.

> **WEB SEARCH**
> The European Travel Commission's website
> www.visiteurope.com
> offers some interesting and unusual themes for holidays ranging across Europe, or within a chosen country.

So much of tourism is packaged and predetermined: others have decided what's good for us, what we should see of their country, what is important and what is insignificant. You can slip through the net of these restrictions by following a path of your own interests.

Although you're unlikely to experience authenticity when a place becomes a manufactured destination, that's not to completely preclude a visit to Disneyland or other mass-tourism attractions. They can be a lot of fun and different from anything at home. But such attractions are entertainment along the way, not insights into a local culture.

WHEN TO GO

With over 220 million visitors each year, Europe is crowded a lot of the time, but the peak summer months of July and August are almost intolerable. Added to the crowds and the peak-time airline and accommodation rates is the fact that in August, Europeans leave the cities in droves, and many attractions close for the main holiday weeks.

Either side – June and September – offers the best weather with less chance of rain, and warmth without oppressive heat. But as July and August fill, the overflow has gone into these months and the crowds are still milling and the prices still high.

That leaves May and October as good months to travel to avoid winter (although I've spent my coldest time ever in Tuscany in October). At these times the crowds are thinner and the prices are lower. Because you're on the edge of the out-of-season period, you'll need to check that your chosen attractions are open. Museums and other attractions often close some days and have reduced hours on others.

The winter months are cold and dark, but the short days and chance of snow are a stark reminder to Australians that they're far from home. Around Christmas time, Europe comes alive with decorations and buskers, busy shoppers and hot chestnuts sold on street corners. The Christmas markets are overwhelming with their range of beautiful produce. After shopping, a glass of hot gluwein will make you feel very European. My first visit to Edinburgh was in the week before Christmas. We arrived in the early evening and walked down the hill towards Princes Street. The streets were strung with small white lights, buskers braved the weather to play carols and the busy shops exhaled warm air. And there, seemingly suspended in the sky, was Edinburgh castle lit up like a fairytale. In the morning we woke to snow.

Although airline prices and accommodation rates normally go up around the weeks of Christmas and New Year, at other times from November to April you can usually pick up good deals.

GATHERING INFORMATION

Nothing beats talking to others who have travelled to your chosen destinations, for their ideas on what to see and what to give a miss. Better still, people who have lived in the cities you're travelling to can give you a deep insight on what to expect.

The internet is an invaluable resource for those who want to self-manage most or all of their travel plans – it has changed the nature of independent travel. But it can be overwhelming and needs a systematic approach to exploration, otherwise you'll be bogged down in the irrelevant and never find your way back to the item of interest you discovered screens ago. (There's information on using the internet throughout this book.)

The countries you plan to visit may have tourism offices in Australia. You can easily check this on the internet, and apply to them for information.

Travel brochures are a good source of information, although much of what they include is replicated on the internet in far more detail. Look for brochures produced by a country's or city's official tourist bureau, as these are primarily concerned with inspiring you to visit, rather than making money from booking the advertised products. As such, they will give more in-depth information about places of interest.

The travel brochures in travel agents are mostly produced by wholesale travel agents who sell the products they represent (hotel rooms, packages, forms of transport) to the consumer via the travel agent. They select products based on commission arrangements with the provider, and volume of business. That is, they dedicate space in their brochures to those products where they expect to make the most sales and profit. This is okay and completely above board, but it usually precludes small, niche businesses that can't achieve a high turnover but can offer a traveller an authentic and personal experience – the essence of getting to know a place.

Some travel agents run information sessions on specific destinations. They usually advertise these sessions in the travel sections of newspapers. And the articles in those travel sections can be terrific, giving some odd bit of information, or a different way to explore a place.

Consumer travel exhibitions can be a colourful and enticing source of information. If you're ready to book, and know exactly what you want, then these events are also great places to pick up a bargain.

Television travel shows can be a guide to a destination. The information is usually superficial because of the limited time dedicated to any one place, but they'll give you a taste of what's available, and will sometimes profile a small, unique business that you'd never otherwise find out about.

TRAVEL TIP
Planning can include such basics as knowing if a public holiday falls during your time in a country. This can either be good because an event is held on that day, or bad because everything will be closed.

READING AS PREPARATION

The more you know about a country in advance, the more satisfying your travels will be. Your knowledge will increase your curiosity to find out more, and will make you more discerning and questioning about what you read and see. You can feel your mind expand to take in the new information that will serve you well on your travels. You choose Spain, for example, and in reading about the country such vaguely known words as Iberia or Andalusia are given meaning and context.

Guidebooks are the most obvious reading matter when preparing for your holiday, and they offer a wealth of information, from currency matters to weather to accommodation and attractions. But they cover so much in a limited space that they can only skim the surface. Where John Julius Norwich takes 600-odd pages to tell the history of Venice, a travel guidebook will condense it into ten pages.

Guidebooks focus on the obvious, so you're often left wondering if countries have anything more than churches and museums to offer. To scratch deeper, good travel writing is an invaluable behind-the-scenes source of knowledge about a place. The best writers will uncover for you what would otherwise take years of living in a country to really understand. For example, Colin Thurbron takes you into the deepest (and at times bleakest) heart of Russia in his book *To Siberia*; *Desiring Italy* (edited by Susan Cahill). It is a passionate and disarming collection of stories by twenty-eight women who know and love that country.

A phrasebook is a good tool for the foreign-language countries that you will be visiting. Even if you only know the basics of 'hello' and 'thank you', your efforts will be appreciated, you'll avoid the stereotype of the arrogant tourist, and learning the lingo is an enjoyable part of preparation. (Try using a language CD in the car. I've driven up and down the highway to Melbourne practising my French, earning odd looks from fellow motorists.)

Google Earth is good for exploring the lay of the land. It might not tell you much about a destination, but it helps to paint a picture and it is fun to follow a mountain range or a coastline to see where it leads.

Libraries offer a world of information: travel books, language books and CDs, histories, biographies, art books, books on national cuisine – in fact, any slant you want to explore about a country or place.

Books and films are wonderful resources for anticipating and expanding the experience of your holiday. Small moments of recognition give untold pleasure. Visiting a Viking long house in Norway is fascinating, but the experience will mean so much more if you've read the history before leaving home. There's something very satisfying about walking down a street in a city you've never visited before, and having a jolt of recognition. It might be while walking in streets of Vienna as portrayed in the movie *The Third Man*, or travelling by gondola along the Grand Canal of Venice just as happened in *The Wings of the Dove*.

TRAVEL TIP

Explore your local library or bookshop for books that will give you a wealth of background knowledge for your travels. Here is a list of some of my favourites. This snapshot will give you an idea of how eclectic your reading can be:

- Europe: Geert Mak's *In Europe* covers 100 years of history across 100 European cities; *A Time of Gifts* by Patrick Leigh Fermor
- Scotland: *The Highland Clearances* by John Prebble
- England: anything by Charles Dickens or Jane Austen; *The Tyrannicide Brief* by Geoffrey Robertson; *Small Island* by Andrea Levy
- Ireland: *The Many-Coloured Land* by Christopher Koch; *Away* by Jane Urquart; *Irish Diary* by Heinrich Böll
- London: *Mrs Dalloway* by Virginia Woolf
- The Netherlands: *Headlong* by Michael Frayn; *Girl with a Pearl Earring* by Tracy Chevalier
- Denmark: *Miss Smilla's Feeling for Snow* by Peter Hoeg
- Norway: *Kristen Lavransdatter* by Sigrid Undset

- Germany: anything by Heinrich Böll; *The Tin Drum* by Günter Grass; Anna Funder's *Stasiland*
- Austria: *The Radetsky March* by Joseph Roth
- Prague: anything by Milan Kundera; *Prague Pictures* by John Banville
- Italy: *Italians* by Barzini Luigi; *I Claudius* and *Claudius the God* by Robert Graves; *The Marble Faun* by Nathaniel Hawthorne
- Venice: *A History of Venice* by John Julius Norwich; *The Wings of the Dove* by Henry James
- Sicily: Giuseppe di Lampedusa's book *The Leopard*; Peter Robb's *Midnight in Sicily*
- France: *Le Belle France* by Alistaire Horne; any biography or history of Napoleon; *A Place of Greater Safety* by Hilary Mantel; *Pére Goriot* by Honoré de Balzac
- Spain: *The Maze of the Muse* by Larry Buttrose; *The Face of Spain* by Gerald Brenan; Ernest Hemingway's classic, *For Whom the Bell Tolls*
- Portugal: José Saramago's *Journey to Portugal*
- Russia: *Peter the Great* by Robert Massie; Malcolm Bradbury's *To the Hermitage*; anything by Ändrei Makine, or Tolstoy of course; *The Master and Margarita* by Mikhail Bulgakov
- The Balkans: *Black Lamb and Grey Falcon* by Rebecca West; *Eastern Approaches* by Fitzroy MacLean
- Turkey: *Istanbul: Memories of a City*, *The Black Book*, and other books by Orhan Pamuk
- Greek Islands: *Mermaid Singing* by Charmian Clift; *Captain Corelli's Mandolin* by Louis de Bernieres; *The House in the Light* by Beverley Farmer
- Corfu: *Corfu* by Robert Dessaix or Lawrence Durell's *Prospero's Cell*
- Egypt: *The Alexandria Quartet* by Lawrence Durell

Beyond the literary, you might like to research the more utilitarian details of a destination. Atlases usually include useful information about geographical, environmental and social issues (make sure your atlas is current, or you'll be studying countries that may no longer exist). The Department of Foreign Affairs and Trade (DFAT) has a section on its website that covers a range of information about 240 countries. The site is mostly trade-related, but it lists countries in alphabetical order and offers political and economic overviews, as well as advice for travellers.

WEB SEARCH

Using **www.amazon.com** you can find different genres of relevant books by following these steps:
- for travel guides: Books > Browse subjects > Travel > type in name of destination (eg *Spain*)
- for travel writing: Books > Browse subjects > Travel > type in *Spanish literature*
- for literature with the destination as a theme: Books > type in *Spanish literature*
- for non-fiction works with the destination as a theme: Books > type in *Spain*

BUILDING ANTICIPATION

Reading books, watching movies, talking to friends, scanning the travel pages of the weekend newspapers – these simple and pleasurable pursuits heighten your sense of anticipation, and anticipation is an important, if often neglected, part of a holiday experience.

Those weeks leading up to the time of departure can be terribly hectic, but somehow you need to clear some space in your mind and time in your day to dedicate to daydreaming about your holiday.

TRAVEL TIP
Some simple ways to build anticipation:
- collect the books you want to read in preparation, and pile them up by your bed
- check the cinema advertisements and TV guides for relevant films to see, or study the DVDs at your local hire shop
- listen to the music that's representative of the places you'll visit, for example flamenco guitar for Spain
- go for a walk in the evening, with your travel partner if possible, and talk about where you're up to and what still needs to be done
- draw up your 'to do' list and stick it on the fridge, and delight in each moment of ticking off another step achieved
- invite friends for dinner who know about the places you plan to visit

- find out about and sample the food and wine of the countries you'll visit
- print some images of places you'll visit (from visitor guide websites for example) and stick them up on the fridge
- visit your local art gallery to see works from the country you will be visiting
- keep the atlas, maps and guidebooks handy, to refer to often
- study the weather for your destinations and start to plan your travel wardrobe

2

GETTING STARTED

A journey of a thousand miles must begin with a single step.

Lao Tzu

- Tools for planning
- The very basics: passports and visas
- Health, safety and travel insurance
- Customs and quarantine
- Elections at home
- Global roaming
- Keeping track
- Using travel agents
- Delightfully different
- Steps towards reservations
- Managing the last moments
- Green planning

TOOLS FOR PLANNING

It can be tempting to book on the spur of the moment. But it's certainly not wise. There is much to be considered and undertaken before you start on the more obvious aspects of travel planning. When you first start, your ideas resemble a tin of buttons, all jumbled up together. Some are bright and shiny and catch your eye, distracting you with their loveliness. Others are dull little black buttons that look boring but are really the most serviceable. You need to work methodically to separate the buttons into their various types, never overlooking the worth of the less attractive.

The checklists in this book will help you to plan, but they will also help you to manage the stress of getting away. Once you've listed what you need to do, pack and so on, you have cleared your mind of all that baggage that weighs you down with anxiety, that you'll forget something important. Checklists give you a systematic and practical step-by-step approach to managing information and tasks. Keep your thoughts free to ponder the joys of expectation, not the worries of forgetting to cancel the newspaper.

The spreadsheets also provide you with a management tool. They guide your steps in planning, help you compare prices, budget, and keep track of your itinerary and bookings.

THE VERY BASICS: PASSPORTS AND VISAS

There was a time when travel was remarkably uncomplicated. Provided you had plenty of time and bucket-loads of money, you could take off on a Grand Tour with little to limit your journey. Thomas Cook started the process of packaging in the mid-1800s, but it wasn't until 1914 that passports became necessary.

Since the end of World War II, there's been a revolution. Tourism has exploded, and travel is no longer the preserve of the wealthy. More recently, dangers both real and exaggerated have become part of the travel scene. Borders are protected against unsuitable people, but have become more permeable to the spread of disease. It's no longer possible to simply pack your trunks, gather your servants and set sail for foreign lands.

> **WEB SEARCH**
> The Department of Foreign Affairs and Trade website's travel pages are invaluable – **www.smartraveller.gov.au** (be careful to type only one 't', and 'gov', not 'com', or you'll end up at commercial websites rather than that of DFAT

Passports

If you have an existing passport, check that it has a minimum of six months' validity from the return date of your travels. You can easily renew a current passport or one that has expired within the last twelve months (more than twelve months and you'll have to apply for a new passport). Conditions and renewal forms are available at **www.passports.gov.au** or through Australia Post. Replacing a lost passport is not the same as renewing your passport – for this you need to start from scratch with a passport application form. To apply for a new passport, follow the steps on **www.passports.gov.au** or apply at an Australian Post outlet.

> **WEB SEARCH**
> For all passport information, go to **www.passports.gov.au**

Allow a minimum of three weeks for renewal or new passports; if you need your passport in less time than this, there is a Priority Processing Service that guarantees a passport within two working days, plus postage time. The processing will be delayed if you don't initially provide the required information, documents and photographs.

The new generation of passports being issued in Australia is the ePassport – a system designed to detect identity fraud using computer chips and biometrics. It works like this: you provide two good-quality photographs, following the guidelines provided in the passport application form. The photographs are digitised and stored in a government database. Your ePassport contains a computer chip holding the image along with your personal information as it appears on the photo page of your passport (name, date of birth, sex etc). When you pass through immigration control, your face, your passport photo and your image on the computer chip can all be compared.

It's not all good news. The process at the airport can be very slow. You look at a camera, which 'reads' your face and tries to match it to the image on the computer chip. The image has to be very close to be recognisable, so you can't smile, and it's probably not a good idea to grow a beard while you're away if your passport photo is beardless.

In addition to the passport photos that you need for your passport application, you might need extra copies if you're applying for visas. It is also worth taking a couple of extra photos with you on your travels, in case you lose your passport and have to have it replaced, or to use, if required, on train or bus passes.

The sad thing about modern technology is that fewer countries are stamping passports, thus robbing we travellers of a memoir of our journeys. However, if you really want a stamp, you can usually ask for one and the customs officers will oblige.

TRAVEL TIP
- Keep your passport safe at all times, including while at home
- Passports are a prime target for theft, so be vigilant in keeping yours safe while travelling; replacing a lost or stolen passport while travelling will disrupt your travel plans
- Keep your passport separate from credit cards and other identity documentation
- If you have an International Drivers Permit, use this wherever possible as proof of identity, rather than extracting your passport from its secure place
- Lost or stolen passports must be reported as soon as possible
  If you lose your passport while overseas, first report the loss to the police, then seek consular assistance
- If you have an existing passport, you don't have to replace it with an ePassport until renewal is due

Visas

A visa is not a passport; it is an official stamp imprinted in your passport, giving you temporary permission from a foreign country to enter that country. There are different visas for different purposes for your visit (such as leisure, business or education). Visas can be for single or multiple entries into a country, and can be limited by the number of days you are permitted to stay in the country, or by an expiry date. Your passport and international flight itinerary are required as part of the documentation when applying for a visa; other support documentation varies from country to country.

Not all countries require visas, but it is important, in these early stages of planning, to check the requirements of each of the countries you plan to visit. Your travel agent can advise you, or you can find the information at **www.smartraveller.gov.au**.

TRAVEL TIP
When looking at dates, for example the expiry date of your visa, check what format they are written in, ie, month/day or day/month. There's a big difference between 1st October as 01/10 and 10th January as 01/10

WEB SEARCH
For visa information on the **www.smartraveller.gov.au** website, follow the prompts: **www.smartraveller.gov.au** > Travel advice > select Destination, eg Russia > scroll down to Entry & Exit requirements > Contact embassy > Index > select Russian Consulate. Contact the consulate direct, using the contact information on the web page

Be aware that some consulates are very slow at issuing visas – they can take from three days up to four weeks or more. The lead time is even longer if you need visas for more than one country. Because your passport is required to issue a visa, you can only apply for one visa at a time. The cost of a visa varies from country to country.

Visalink has a website where you can apply for visas online. The site allows you to check if you need a visa, the types of visas a country offers, and how long the application is likely to take. There is an easy step-by-step application form, but you still need to send your passport away for the insertion of the visa stamp.

WEB SEARCH
For visas online: **www.visalink.com.au**
You can also find visa information at **www.qantas.com.au**

Dual nationality
It is possible to have a dual nationality (Australian and something else) without knowing it. It may be through birth, marriage, state succession, or a range of other ways as determined by different countries. If you have any suspicion that you could be a dual

national, find out before travelling, as this may have consequences if you travel to the country of your other nationality. Visit the DFAT website, **www.dfat.gov.au/protocol/DiplomaticList**, to contact the relevant foreign embassy and make your inquiries with them.

> **WEB SEARCH**
> Other Australian citizenship issues can be raised with the Department of Immigration and Citizenship via their website: www.immi.gov.au

HEALTH, SAFETY AND TRAVEL INSURANCE

The facts can't be avoided: about 18 per cent of travellers lose at least one day of their travels to illness, and nearly 4 per cent lose four or more days. Some illnesses can be avoided with common sense; others could see you in hospital with mounting medical bills.

> **TRAVEL TIP**
> Three steps in your early planning:
> - get fit, keep healthy
> - find out if you need vaccinations six to twelve weeks prior to travelling
> - purchase travel insurance

Planning for your holiday should include aiming to be as well and as fit to travel as possible – it will greatly enhance your holiday enjoyment. Travel always involves a lot of walking, even in cities, and you don't want to wait till you're away to find you aren't fit enough to manage the walking easily. Your plans might include a medical check-up and an exercise program.

Vaccinations

There's a very helpful website maintained by the US Department of Health and Human Services – the Centres for Disease Control and Prevention (**www.cdc.gov**). Here you can search by destination for health information, required and recommended vaccinations, and likely health and disease risks. Two Australian websites that also offer good advice for travellers are **www.travelclinic.com.au** and **www.traveldoctor.com.au**. They provide information about vaccinations along with the latest health alerts, and a list of clinics in Australia that offer medical services especially for intending travellers.

> **WEB SEARCH**
> Websites for vaccinations, health warnings and other health information:
> World Health Organization:
> www.who.int/ith/en
> www.travelclinic.com.au
> www.traveldoctor.com.au
> Centres for Disease Control and Prevention:
> wwwn.cdc.gov/travel

Travel insurance

Travel insurance is a non-negotiable travel requirement: you simply cannot afford to travel overseas without it. Lost luggage can spoil your holiday; a hospital bill can ruin your future.

You can purchase travel insurance from a wide range of suppliers: your existing insurer, your bank, your travel agent and through airline websites. Some credit cards have a built-in benefit of free travel insurance if you purchase a portion of your travel arrangements using that card. Ask your bank manager for details. If you use this service keep in mind the following:

- you must satisfy the terms required to activate the insurance cover
- no policy is issued – the policy is between the bank and the insurer. This means that you have no hard-copy proof of travel insurance while you are away, so it is imperative that you travel with the insurance company's contact details
- you need to print out the full policy from your bank's website and read it carefully to ensure you are covered for all possible eventualities

> **WEB SEARCH**
> You can compare insurance costs across the major brands at
> www.travelinsurance.com.au

TRAVEL TIP
Things to check regarding your travel insurance:
- that it is activated if you are using the insurance associated with your credit card
- that it covers you in all the countries you plan to visit
- that it covers at least the basics of ambulance, hospital treatment and medical evacuation
- that it also covers general medical expenses including existing medical conditions
- that it covers you for any adventure activities in which you plan to participate
- that it covers death overseas, including the return of remains to Australia
- that you know what the policy excludes, for example types of circumstances and activities
- that you know if the insurance company pays the medical expenses direct, or if you have to pay and seek reimbursement

Make sure you take the insurer's contact details with you in the event that you need to make a claim while you are away.

Reciprocal health-care agreements
Take your Medicare card with you to the following countries, where Australia has reciprocal health-care agreements:
- Finland
- Italy
- Norway
- Ireland
- Malta
- Netherlands
- New Zealand
- Sweden
- United Kingdom

If you need urgent medical attention in any of these countries you are covered under Medicare. You must alert the doctor or hospital prior to treatment that you wish to take advantage of the reciprocal arrangements.

The reciprocal arrangements don't cover you for health problems that arise during travel to and from one of these countries.

> **WEB SEARCH**
> Details of reciprocal health care agreements can be found at www.medicareaustralia.gov.au

Other medical considerations

Prescriptions issued by your doctor in Australia cannot be filled overseas, so ensure you take sufficient supplies for your needs. If you're taking prescription medications with you, especially if they are Pharmaceutical Benefits Scheme drugs, take a doctor's letter to confirm that the medications are for your personal use, or complete a PBS Medicine Export Declaration form, available from the Health Insurance Commission. Also check that the medications you are taking are legal in the countries you are visiting – ask at the country's embassy.

If you depend on spectacles, ask your optometrist to give you a prescription that can be filled if you lose or damage your glasses while travelling. Taking an old or spare pair of glasses is a good fallback.

Travel alerts

The Australian Government monitors and categorises destinations depending on how safe or otherwise they are for travellers. The DFAT uses five levels of alert, ranging from the common-sense safety approach to all travel (1), through to advice not to travel to a destination (5). You should check the level that applies to the countries you wish to travel to as one of your earliest planning steps. Be aware that your travel insurance may become invalid if you ignore warnings at level 4 (reconsider your need to travel) and level 5 (advised not to travel).

TRAVEL TIP

Use the DFAT website for travellers (www.smartraveller.gov.au):
- subscribing to their email broadcasts that advise of the latest travel alerts
- registering your intention to travel (dates and destinations) along with your contact details

CUSTOMS AND QUARANTINE

On the Australian Customs Service website you can print out an informative brochure that gives details of what you can and cannot take out of or bring into Australia.

WEB SEARCH
- Customs' brochure is downloadable at **www.customs.gov.au**
- see other countries' embassy websites to check what they will allow. Click through from **www.smartraveller.gov.au**
- the Qantas website has stacks of good information under Flying with us > Before you travel. Go to Country Information and check what quarantine and other rules apply at your destination countries

It's good to know in advance what you can return home with, so that you don't purchase gifts that never see beyond the airport. Banned animal and plant products might include skins, or wooden masks, or herbal teas. Some goods can be treated, but there is a fee for this service.

Goods exported in passenger baggage

If you are taking away with you a laptop computer, camera or other item that may appear on return to be something you have purchased duty free, you can fill out a Goods Exported in Passenger Baggage form (available on Customs' website), declaring that the goods are owned by you. You hand this form, with the goods and your passport, to the customs officer as you leave Australia. Once registered, you need to retain the form, so you don't have to declare the goods on return.

ELECTIONS AT HOME

If there is to be an election while you are away, you can still vote. However, if you fail to vote, you won't be fined. You will receive a letter from the Australian Electoral Commission (AEC) asking why you didn't vote, and your explanation of being overseas will be a legitimate reason. Alternatively, you can inform the AEC of your intended travels before you leave.

There are three ways in which you can vote, provided you are on the electoral role:

1. In person: once an election is called, the AEC will post a list of overseas polling places on their website at which you can vote in person (if the place is handy)
2. Postal vote: once an election is called you can download and print a postal vote application form from the AEC website, but you cannot vote electronically. You must post or fax the completed form to your nearest overseas polling place. The process varies for state and territory elections, so contact the appropriate electoral office (you'll find a list of links on the AEC site)
3. Vote ahead: just prior to an election, the AEC sets up pre-poll centres at some Australian airports where you can vote before leaving for your overseas trip.

> **WEB SEARCH**
> Go to www.aec.gov.au for information on federal elections. Click through from this site for state and territory electoral commissions

CHECKLISTS

As you go through each of these early steps, make a list of emergency and other contact details to take with you. It's worthwhile entering the phone numbers into your mobile phone.

For general problems:

- ❑ lost passport (consular offices)
- ❑ travel insurance claim (insurer's phone number)
- ❑ lost credit cards (bank's phone number)
- ❑ lost airline tickets (airline phone numbers)
- ❑ travel problems (your travel agent's number)
- ❑ email problems (your internet service provider's contact details)
- ❑ mobile phone difficulties (your carrier's phone number)
- ❑ travel details (the telephone numbers of your accommodation and transport providers)

For emergencies (for more details, see p 161–162):

- ❑ DFAT's emergency numbers in Canberra
- ❑ consular offices for each country
- ❑ your 'in case of emergency' (ICE) numbers
- ❑ the relevant emergency numbers that apply in each country

Also, take two photocopies of the following documents – take one set with you (kept separate from the originals) and leave one with your family or friends at home:

- ❑ passport photo page
- ❑ visas
- ❑ travel insurance policy
- ❑ driver's licence
- ❑ credit cards
- ❑ traveller's cheques (record the numbers)
- ❑ phone cards
- ❑ itinerary
- ❑ completed accommodation details spreadsheet (see p 94)

GLOBAL ROAMING

To use your mobile phone overseas, you need to ask your contract to activate global roaming (at least in those countries that use the same system as Australia). Contact your carrier well in advance of your travel date. For your travels, you will need to take the following:
- a printout of the user guide from your supplier's website
- the instructions for your mobile phone
- guides for your destination countries (the list of carriers and their call rates)
- the contact phone number of your carrier, in case you encounter difficulties with using the service while travelling

TRAVEL TIP

If you use your Australian mobile phone overseas in association with a phone card you will still incur the global roaming fee of around $2 to $3 per minute

KEEPING TRACK

As you start to plan your holiday you will quickly amass a vast amount of information – so much that it's easy to lose your way. You follow link after link on the internet, and find a fabulous cottage on an island in Finland, then you move on – never to find the page with the cottage again. So right at the beginning, it's worth spending a little time setting up a filing system to keep track of information, in a form that makes it manageable and easy to find.

On Google, Bookmarks will help you manage the links to the sites you want to revisit. You can do the same organising with Favourites, but the benefit of Bookmarks is that access to your selected links is not limited to one computer, so you can check your sites while travelling. To be able to do this, you'll need to open a Google account, which is self-explanatory on the site, and free.

Once you have an account, think about the folders you want to create. Bookmarks gives you two tiers – a file (ie a heading/topics) and its contents (ie individual website addresses).

TRAVEL TIP

An example of organising Bookmarks:

File	Contents (example)
General information	smartraveller visalink visiteurope
Airlines	Qantas Singapore Ryanair Easyjet
Airports	Melbourne Heathrow
Other transport	Eurail ICE Germany timetables Seat61 aferry.to
Germany general	Official visitor guide What's on
Frankfurt accommodation	(range of sites that look interesting)
Heidelberg accommodation	(range of sites that look interesting)
Spain general	Official visitor guide sites about history
Barcelona accommodation	(range of sites that look interesting)

TRAVEL TIP

When visiting websites written in foreign languages, look for the English translation button. It's usually in the form of a small British flag.

Don't let your bookmarks become unwieldy. Delete the links to sites when you no longer need them.

Add a currency conversion site to your Favourites to easily check prices in international currencies. When you're checking accommodation and other prices, open a second browser window and click on your currency conversion site. Leave this open as you check prices, moving between the two browsers to convert rates to Australian dollars.

> **WEB SEARCH**
> One of many currency conversion websites:
> www.xe.com/ucc/

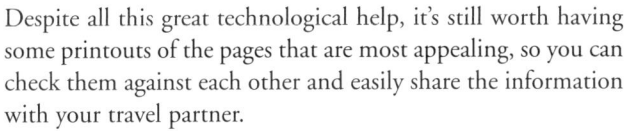

Despite all this great technological help, it's still worth having some printouts of the pages that are most appealing, so you can check them against each other and easily share the information with your travel partner.

For this reason, start a hard-copy folder and use dividers for topics such as transport, accommodation, vouchers, entertainment, documentation and so on. When deciding on accommodation, print out the home pages of the most likely candidates, and write the town and the check-in and check-out dates in large letters across the top so they are easily identifiable. Attach hard copies of your email correspondence with each. Once you've made your selection, attach confirmation letters, acknowledgement of payment and any other useful information (such as directions to the accommodation). Discard all the sheets you no longer need, and keep the pages of the places you have booked to take away with you.

Also print out those pages you'll need while travelling, such as train timetables, and Google street maps.

USING TRAVEL AGENTS

Travel agents are like a filter – all that product out there in the world comes down a pipe, ever narrowing until it gets strained through the mesh and handed on to the consumer. Along the way there are the various 'middlemen' of the travel industry, and it's worth understanding who does what and how it all comes together.

Individual operator/product: this is the person or business 'on the ground' who runs the accommodation, transport, tour, activity or any other product in the tourism mix.

Chain operator or franchiser: a large business responsible for the marketing (mostly) of many properties or franchises (for example Big 4 tourist parks, Quality Inn, etc). The chain operator charges the member operator a fee for the use of the corporate brand, for advertising and for representing the operator to wholesalers and travel agents. The chain operator will often have quality control guidelines in place, which members are required to follow.

Wholesaler: the company that develops and packages a collection of products, normally in the form of a brochure. Customers of the wholesaler can be travel agents buying on behalf of their clients, or a consumer can go directly to a wholesaler. Wholesalers are normally located in the consumer's country. They don't have any control over the quality of the individual operator, but generally know a considerable amount about the countries they represent.

Inbound travel operator (ITO): the company that finds products for the wholesaler to package. The ITO is normally located in the country of the product (the country to which the consumer is travelling). They are knowledgeable about both the country and the individual operators. In some cases the wholesaler and the ITO are the same company.

Travel agent or retailer: the person or company that sells directly to a consumer, either using the wholesaler's brochure or hunting out relevant individual operators. Travel agents can be independent companies, franchisees or branches of major retail chains.

Who pays whom?

No matter at what level you enter, you'll pay the individual operator's price. From this, the travel agent, the wholesaler and the ITO will each take a commission, which is usually 10 per cent each. The income received by the individual operator will be 100 per cent if the consumer books direct, or between 70 and 90 per cent of their rack rate, depending on how many middlemen are involved in the transaction.

Choosing a travel agent

Like any industry, the travel industry can be cutthroat, and the big players certainly dominate the field. But this does not necessarily make them the best choice. Many travel agents have 'preferred products' – products from whom they receive a bigger commission in return for their recommendation. In some of the large chain retailers you will only ever be offered preferred products, but the product that is the best deal for the travel agent may not be the best deal for you. At present, there is no legal requirement in Australia for travel agents to declare this conflict of interest.

> **WEB SEARCH**
> www.afta.com.au is the official website of the Australian Federation of Travel Agents.
> Have a look at the code of ethics required of travel agents, so you can be alert to suspect practices

Small, independent travel agents are more likely to give you unbiased options, selling products without fear or favour because they are not tied to chains. But small agents can still be swayed by the incentives of gifts, free travel and higher than normal commissions from some products – all working against the consumer getting the very best advice. So ask your travel agent if the product they are recommending is the agency's preferred product, or why they are recommending one product over another.

Some of the most professional travel agents are those who focus on business travel. If you work for a company that uses a travel agent, and they do a good job, try that agent first. If you travel frequently for business, the travel agent will already know many of your travel preferences. Most corporate travel agents are not aligned with preferred products.

If your travels are confined to one region, you're better off using a wholesaler who specialises in that region. They are the same people who the travel agent will contact on your behalf to seek advice and develop a package, so you might as well go directly to the primary source of information. There is generally no price advantage of choosing one or the other as wholesalers won't undercut travel agents who are their main source of business.

The one time you'll be able to get special deals with wholesalers is at consumer travel shows.

> **WEB SEARCH**
> You can find wholesalers on the industry website (the Council of Australian Tour Operators): **www.cato.asn.au**

The best wholesalers to use are those who control the ground content (ie accommodation, tours) at a destination, because that means they have control over the quality of products. You'll need to ask wholesalers how they ensure quality control – a good question for travel agents, too.

When to use a travel agent

In Australia, all travel agents and wholesalers must be accredited. Booking through an accredited travel agent gives you consumer protection and access to the Travel Compensation Fund in the event that a booking for which you have paid a travel agent cannot go ahead. It might be that a hotel has closed without notice or a tour operator has gone broke. Even airlines can fail – think of Ansett and how its demise caused financial loss for travellers.

Other reasons to use a travel agent:
- if your travel arrangements are complicated (lots of connections, multiple countries)
- if you want an itinerary created for you – it's a one-stop-shop for transport, accommodation, tours and restaurants
- so you have a contact if things go wrong
- if you need advice about visas, health warnings and travel insurance
- they'll issue, along with your tickets, the necessary customs forms (although these are also readily available at the airport)
- if you want a flight booking held for a short period of time before final confirmation and payment

- to take advantage of their experience (travel agents are in the game because they love to travel – and they do travel extensively)
- if you want to use transfers (that is, to have someone waiting for you at the end of your long flight, to guide you through the airport, so it doesn't matter how exhausted or bewildered you are when you arrive at your destination)
- if you have a travel agent you have used before and you trust, an agent who is helpful and willing to explore options for you
- if you are concerned about changes to travel alerts, your travel agent is responsible for alerting you to DFAT travel warnings that may affect your plans and insurance cover

Find a good travel agent, and measure their worth by their independence, intimate knowledge of destinations and willingness to hunt out the unusual for you. As a rule of thumb, small is good (both travel agents and wholesalers).

There's some evidence that after the honeymoon of using the internet to plan holidays, there is a drift back to travel agents. There was a perceived price disadvantage with using a travel agent, but this is no longer the case. Apart from special offers made from time to time by operators, the published rate (the 'rack' rate) doesn't vary, irrespective of how you book.

When it's better to book direct

There are situations where it makes more sense for you to book your travel plans directly with the operator, especially when you have the time and internet skills for a thorough exploration of what's available:

- if your arrangements are straightforward – the internet makes it so easy to book point-to-point transport, including car hire
- if you're looking for individual, niche businesses – many small businesses don't have the margins to afford the high commission rates, so you'll never find them through travel agents. If a business is small, it doesn't generate sufficient volume for the ITOs to be interested, so the product doesn't

get brochured and information never filters down the line to wholesalers or travel agents
- if you know the operator (if you've booked with them before, or they've been recommended by a friend)
- if you're looking for special deals

DELIGHTFULLY DIFFERENT

If you elect to put in the hard work of finding accommodation yourself, there are many gems out there to be discovered. On our most recent trip, we had accommodation that was both idiosyncratic and disarmingly lovely.

In Granada we stayed in a cave house. The caves of Sacromonte were once occupied by gypsies but are slowly being restored and renovated for modern living. This is the area in which flamenco music and dance was born.

The cave fronts are startling in their whitewash, reflecting the harsh Andalusian sunshine and shimmering against the blue sky. Our cave was magical, painted white throughout with brightly coloured Spanish furnishings. It had everything we needed but especially a sun-drenched terrace where we took all of our meals gazing across the Darra Valley to the greenly wooded opposite slope that hid the Sierra Nevada from view. Further along the Sabika stands the mighty Alhambra, rising in pink majesty along the crest of the hill.

Next door lived a gypsy couple who spoke only in deep-voiced shouts and who shared their cave with numerous children, four dogs and an indeterminate number of hens. The raucousness added a noisy authenticity to the location.

In Toledo we stayed at one of the Spanish Paradores. In the early 1900s the Spanish government started a program of buying up palaces and turning them over to accommodation for travellers. These days, they provide exquisite accommodation and usually specialise in the local cuisine. The Toledo Paradore, which had been a 14th century palace, looks across to the next hill on which rises the glorious ancient town. Sitting on the balcony sipping sangrias in the early evening, the view was fairytale beautiful.

After this, we stayed in an original 'La Mancha' style windmill just south of Lisbon. Set high on a hill to catch the wind, the windmill (or moinho) offered sweeping views to the vast Rio Sado. Although the grindstones and the windmill blades were gone (thank goodness, we didn't have to duck each time we passed through the front door), there was still plenty of evidence of its working life.

Such places are fun and unusual, add flavour to holiday experiences, and give a true taste of the past – a sense of living in someone else's history.

STEPS TOWARDS RESERVATIONS

The following two chapters offer advice and information for reserving transport and accommodation. To guide you in the complex art of bringing all your travel plans together, use the checklist below, which is set out in chronological order in an attempt to alert you to what needs to be done first, before other steps can be taken. There are also some crosschecks along the way. Tick off each step as it is accomplished (delete those that are irrelevant to your travel plans), so you can easily see if you have forgotten anything.

CHECKLISTS

The following information is available in spreadsheet format on The Five Mile Press website.

- ❏ Decide when you're going to travel
- ❏ Decide how much you can afford to spend
- ❏ Check that your passport is valid/apply for a passport
- ❏ Search destinations, check suitability for time of travel, travel warnings
- ❏ Check if you need a visa
- ❏ Check that long-haul flights are available and within budget; check the cheapest days to travel
- ❏ Get quotes on long-haul flights
- ❏ Search internet for cheap flight destinations; check availability, price, airport location

- [ ] Check that the transport you need (train, ferry, coach) between destinations is available when you need it
- [ ] Make firm decisions about destinations
- [ ] Start your itinerary spreadsheet giving date ranges to each destination
- [ ] Check that the major sights you want to visit are open on the days you will be in town
- [ ] Apply for visas as required
- [ ] Check accommodation options for each destination, email properties for availability and quote
- [ ] Use the accommodation comparison spreadsheet to keep track and make decisions
- [ ] Email selected accommodation to confirm dates and price, and ask for the reservation to be held for a few days (best give a specific date)
- [ ] Check car hire options for each destination required
- [ ] Use car hire comparison spreadsheet to keep track and make decisions
- [ ] Check availability and price of other transport needs
- [ ] Complete first draft of itinerary spreadsheet
- [ ] Complete the first draft of your budget spreadsheet, allowing for food, shopping and contingencies
- [ ] Check on itinerary spreadsheet that you have accounted for all nights and all travel needs
- [ ] Check travel insurance arrangements
- [ ] Book flights; if with a travel agent, agree on final confirmation/payment date
- [ ] Purchase travel insurance as required
- [ ] Book short-haul flights, include details on itinerary spreadsheet
- [ ] Purchase other transport tickets, eg Eurail; mark days of train travel on itinerary spreadsheet
- [ ] Confirm accomodation, pay as required, record on itinerary spreadsheet
- [ ] Book car hire as required
- [ ] Update budget spreadsheet with flights, insurance, transport, car hire and accommodation, check you are still within budget

- ❏ Pay travel agent for long-haul flights on due date
- ❏ When tickets arrive, check all details against itinerary spreadsheet
- ❏ Search what entertainment and activities are on in each destination, purchase tickets as required, add to itinerary checklist
- ❏ Review your budget
- ❏ Use your itinerary spreadsheet to crosscheck all dates against tickets and confirmations for flights, accommodation, transport, car hire
- ❏ Ensure all voucher details and payments are recorded on the itinerary spreadsheet
- ❏ Prepare your accommodation details spreadsheet details with addresses, phone numbers, directions, check in and check out times, and any special instructions
- ❏ Create a safe place to store documents, tickets, vouchers and paperwork

TRAVEL TIP

Buy tickets in advance to major events, including blockbuster exhibitions at art galleries where an advance booking will get you in past the queuing crowds.

MANAGING THE LAST MOMENTS

The last couple of days before you travel can be the most stressful. Here are some domestic 'to do' lists for the fridge door.

CHECKLIST

The last couple of weeks before you depart

- ❏ arrange cancellation of newspapers
- ❏ arrange collection of mail
- ❏ ask neighbours to water the pots and garden
- ❏ book the dog/cat into the kennel
- ❏ print out mailing labels for those to whom you plan to send postcards (this is an easy way of ensuring you don't forget anyone, or go away without their address)

- ❏ shop in a way that ensures you have finished everything in the fridge before leaving
- ❏ ask a friend to start your car from time to time
- ❏ pay all the accounts and arrange payment of those that will fall due while you are away

On the day before departure

- ❏ check and record the latest currency exchange rates applicable for your destination
- ❏ empty and defrost the freezer (if you're turning off the power, which is good for saving emissions)
- ❏ empty, clean and turn off the fridge
- ❏ soak the pot plants, take out the indoor plants
- ❏ book your taxi to the airport
- ❏ leave your travel itinerary (with addresses and contact details) with a family member or friend
- ❏ change your message on your phone's message bank, and perhaps activate an email automatic reply as well
- ❏ check the weather forecast on the internet for the city you are travelling to

On the day of departure

- ❏ empty the dustbin
- ❏ turn off all taps tightly
- ❏ turn off the hot water, or all water to the house
- ❏ turn off the power or, if you need it for your security system, ensure you've turned off all appliances at the power points
- ❏ turn off gas bottles (domestic, barbecue)
- ❏ check that all windows and doors are locked
- ❏ leave a key with a neighbour
- ❏ leave a car key as ranged

GREEN PLANNING

If travel were to be no more than tacky souvenirs and a fistful of photographs, then the burden on the environment is unforgivable. But if it can nurture tolerance through exposing one culture to another, challenging preconceived opinions and prejudices, increasing understanding of differences, then perhaps we can still see it as a balance on the other side of the environmental scales. There are 6.6 billion strangers out there in the world. Getting to know some of them makes it far more difficult to be intolerant and hostile.

There are suggestions through this book on how to lessen your impact on the environment when travelling. Here are some early considerations:

- create your own carbon credit trading scheme: be additionally conservative at home to take account for the extra impact of your travels
- search for accommodation and travel businesses that have green credentials
- turn off your home's power and hot water heater while you're away
- travel to consume experiences, not resources
- bring home memories, not products
- make conservation a point of honour throughout your travels

3

AIR AND GROUND: GETTING AROUND

*For my part, I travel not to go anywhere,
but to go. I travel for travel's sake.
The great affair is to move.*

Robert Louis Stevenson

- In the air
- Train and coach travel
- On the road
- Take to the water
- Exploring locally
- Travelling green

IN THE AIR

Starting with long-haul flights

Your long-haul flight is likely to be the most expensive part of your holiday, and the departure and return dates will dictate everything else, so this is where your transport planning needs to begin. Quite a while in advance, start watching the websites of the major airlines from which you will select your carrier. Check around the days you want to fly out and return, and see what the price ranges are around those dates. You'll be surprised how much the prices can vary within a week, and from week to week.

TRAVEL TIP
Some airlines offer seniors discounts – they just don't advertise the fact. It's always worth checking. You might not find it on the website, so give the airline a call.

There are any number of websites that help you search for the best airfare, and the technology is getting more and more sophisticated. The site **www.farecast.com** not only gives availability and prices, it also monitors trends and gives predictions of the best time to buy. Airlines monitor forward bookings and issues that may influence decisions to travel, and adjust their prices accordingly. This website uses similar information to monitor whether prices are likely to go up or down. At present it only covers USA destinations, but watch this space.

WEB SEARCH
For flight price comparisons, try **www.webjet.com**.
There are dozens of flight comparison websites, but many of them are travel agents with preferred product arrangements

TRAVEL TIP
Check airline websites for a host of information beyond just flights, including travelling with a disability, documentation needs and avoiding deep vein thrombosis, as well as links to information about destinations, accommodation, car hire, insurance, and more.

Travel agents perform a number of invaluable roles, but for me, their biggest benefit is that they will book a flight and hold it for an agreed period of time while you bring all the other aspects of your travel into line (such as confirm other flights or accommodation). If you book your flight on the internet you'll have to pay immediately to confirm it. Be aware, however, that travel agents vary enormously in how hard they will work for you. If you ask for a particular date, some will just book that date; others will advise you if there's a seasonal rate change or special offer close to your dates. If you're booking at the last minute, some will merely shrug and tell you all flights are completely full; others will go like terriers to find you a seat. Even when using a travel agent, it is still worthwhile researching dates and prices on the internet, so that you can speak knowledgeably and be alert to prices that don't sound right.

TRAVEL TIP
This is vitally important: your name as it appears on your ticket must be identical to how it appears in your passport, otherwise the airline can refuse you access to your flight.

When your tickets arrive from the travel agent or airline (including e-tickets), immediately check that all the details are correct, and check against your itinerary. Then check again. A mistake can really mess up your holiday.

CHECKLIST
Check your tickets for the following:

- [ ] your name (how it appears on the ticket compared with how it appears in your passport)
- [ ] dates and times of every leg
- [ ] taxes paid
- [ ] luggage allowances
- [ ] airports and terminals
- [ ] destinations and stopovers

Make sure that, as part of the booking process, the airline is given the mobile phone number that you'll be travelling with so that they can advise you of delayed departures, cancellations or changes to security measures. Check their website on the day before a long-haul flight to ensure nothing has happened to change the circumstances of your flight.

TRAVEL TIP
If you have special needs, register these with the airline at the time of booking, or as soon as possible thereafter. With most airlines you can make special requests or changes to your booking online, including the following:
- inform them of special dietary needs (usually a minimum of twenty-four hours in advance for most special meals, and thirty-six hours for kosher meals)
- ask for a specific seat reservation (the time that seat reservations

are 'open' can be very brief and unpredictable and not always available on the airline's website)
- organise to send sporting equipment as luggage
- advise the airline of upgrades, cancellations or other changes
- advise the airline of changes to your contact details

Check-in time for international flights departing from Australia is from 120 to sixty minutes before the flight. If you arrive less than sixty minutes before departure you may be denied access to your flight. Check-in times at other international airports vary, and can change with world events, so find out from your airline close to your departure date.

TRAVEL TIP
Most airlines deliberately over-book flights, knowing from experience the percentage of 'no show' passengers. Sometimes their calculations go awry and there are more passengers than seats – another good reason to check in early.

All seats are not created equal
You would not fly economy if you could afford business or first-class travel. But if you're going to be confined to the back of the plane, you can at least do some homework to try to secure one of the better seats.

First is the issue of aisle versus window seats in the side rows. There are positives and negatives to both.

If you're on the aisle:
- you can get up and down without disturbing anyone else
- you'll have one arm rest that you don't have to share
- you can stretch your legs into the aisle (but don't leave them there)
- you'll have to suffer others climbing over you
- you risk having your elbow knocked by a passing trolley or passenger

In a window seat:
- you have the enjoyment of watching take-off and landing, and somewhere interesting to look when the movie is boring

- you have a greater chance of uninterrupted sleep with no-one clambering over you
- you can rest your head against the window
- you will have to climb over others to get out

The side middle seat on a Boeing 747 has nothing good to offer, unless you have your partner on one side.

The only good thing about the middle row of seats is the fact that this is where the empty seats are on those rare flights that aren't fully booked. Like you, your fellow passengers will be waiting anxiously for the exit doors to close before springing into an empty row to claim it for themselves for a chance to stretch out and sleep.

Some other points to consider:
- seats towards the front of the plane (in front of the engines) are quieter than those behind the wings
- there's more noise and traffic close to the galley and toilets
- seats at bulkheads, or partitions, can be good on some planes, but on others they will have less pitch (leg room), or seats that don't recline
- exit rows are highly coveted, but to get these seats, you have to prove to the airline check-in staff that you are fit to assist in the case of an emergency (the seats can't be reserved in advance)
- at the back of a Boeing 747, where the plane tapers, the last few rows on either side have only two seats – good for two travelling together
- airlines go to a lot of trouble to develop ergonomically sound seats, so they're most comfortable when you sit in them properly, with your bottom well back in the seat
- most seats now have adjustable headrests that wrap around and allow you to rest your head to the side

There are some informative websites that show the seating configurations on all the different types of planes. You can check what seating is best on the models you'll be flying in, and at the time of booking your flight you can use the knowledge you've gleaned from the websites to request a seat reservation. For some international flights, you can request seat reservations online or by phoning the airline, but the timing varies from weeks prior if the flight is full, up to the departure day. Remember that having a seat reservation does not mean you are checked in, or that your seat is guaranteed if you arrive late for check in.

> **WEB SEARCH**
> Websites to check seating arrangements include
> www.seatguru.com and www.seatexpert.com

How to survive a long-haul flight

Nothing is more symbolic of escape and excitement than the pushback of an aircraft, the moments of slightly sweaty palms, then the whoosh forwards and upwards, towards a new destination. The power and tension of take-off is the culmination of all the anticipation and planning, a physical metaphor for the uplifting experiences that await you.

TRAVEL TIP
While most people try to look cool and well travelled by ostentatiously not watching the safety demonstration conducted by the cabin crew, there are some things you will always need to be aware of no matter how often you fly, such as the location of the exits.

Having climbed into the heavens and scanned the duty-free magazines and menu card, there's the risk of tedium creeping into this very early stage of your holiday. But it doesn't have to be like that. Holidays are not just about arriving and doing; to get the most from your time away, the journey needs to hold its own value. Long-haul travel can be a drag – or you can look at it as one of the rare opportunities in life when you're faced with many hours without any calls on your time. It's stretching the point, perhaps, to praise the food in economy class, but even this can have its own appeal, delivered as it is at regular intervals to break the flight into manageable chunks of time – and no-one asks you to do the dishes.

Planning to make long-haul flights bearable, if not enjoyable, is not unlike creating your 'to do' list at work to allow you to get through the tasks of the day. It's a matter of creating a menu of activities for your flight. The planning starts long before you arrive at the airport. If you're a reader, take time to select a book that will be a treat to read. It might be a thriller: something racy but not so light or short that you'll be finished before Hong Kong. Or perhaps this is your chance to make a start on *War and Peace*, or *The Mill on the Floss*. Make sure it's a book that you know has had good reviews, or has been recommended by a friend whose reading taste you share. There's nothing worse than realising half an hour into the flight that you're not going to enjoy the book you've chosen. Magazines are okay for moments during the trip, but I find they don't hold my attention sufficiently to allow the hours to fly past.

If possible, arrange for your holiday to start on the day before you travel, and create a mindset that that day is the beginning of your holiday, starting the wind-down process even though it will involve last-minute preparations. A day without the pressure of work getting in the way of final preparations will put you in better shape to relax during the flight.

The day before you travel, drink plenty of water, eat low-fat foods and try to avoid alcohol, so your system is primed for relaxation. Stay up as late as possible the night before, so you will be more inclined to sleep on the flight.

When you go to bed on that final night at home, plan to be completely ready to leave the next day – bags packed, clothes laid out ready to be put on (having selected comfortable clothes and shoes for the flight – see Chapter 6), passports, tickets, itineraries all accounted for and safely stowed.

Once on the coach from Bairnsdale to Melbourne, we were only a few minutes out of Bairnsdale when there was a scream from the back of the bus. A woman had just realised that she'd left her passport at home. The coach driver was very cool. 'Where do you live, lady?' he asked, and took the coach rumbling through the back streets of the town to the woman's home, where she dashed inside to retrieve her passport. That's country Australia for you, but few people can rely on this sort of service, so make sure you have all your paperwork in order well before you leave.

Arrive at the airport with plenty of time to spare. Checking in to your flight as soon as the appropriate desk opens might marginally increase your chance of an exit row seat, or at least your choice of window or aisle seat, but there are other benefits. For one, you'll feel more in control, and it's another opportunity to start to slow down. Once you've checked in, move through security and immigration, and be sure you know where your flight gate is located. Then you can comb the duty-free shops in that aimless way of travellers, or hunt for the items you've planned to purchase, or you can settle down with your phrasebook to learn the lingo of the country to which you're flying.

When your flight is called, don't rush. There are another few hundred people getting on board, so there's little point in standing in a long queue or rushing to get into the seat you will be forced to occupy for the next nine hours. You might miss out on the locker directly overhead, but if you've planned your time on board and have little cabin luggage, this shouldn't matter. So take your time.

Once on board, settle in to this space that is yours alone: book here, water bottle there, lip salve in pocket, valuables placed safely (including when you're asleep). After all, this is home now for quite a stretch. Then go to the in-flight magazine to see what movies are on for your flight, and decide what you'll watch and when. Schedule them around meals, reading, sleeping and simply daydreaming about all that is to come.

TRAVEL TIP
Plan your flight around what's happening on board:
- soon after takeoff, there's usually a bar service
- following that, the first meal is served (food is loaded into the ovens prior to takeoff and cooking starts soon after the seatbelt sign is switched off)
- after the meal service, there's usually a rush for the toilets
- after this, the lights are dimmed and cabin crew leave passengers undisturbed to get some rest
- during the 'night' the crew pass up and down the aisles with juice,

water, sometimes snack packs and fruit
- timing for the last meal depends on whether it's a main meal or a snack, but either will be completed in time to allow for a last minute toilet rush before descent
- Boeing has developed new mood lighting technology to replicate the day cycle. As this is introduced to planes, the sequence of service may change

When you're ready to sleep, go through your normal bedtime routine – wash, clean your teeth, perhaps do some stretching exercises, then arrange your 'bed' – shape your headrest, recline your seat, plump up your pillow, tuck in the blanket. Wax earplugs are more comfortable to use than the plastic ones supplied on board; the eye mask will help to replicate a dark night. Then turn off your light: sweet dreams, if you're lucky.

If you can't sleep, don't worry. If you have a window seat, there's something wonderfully mesmerising about watching all those countries shrouded in darkness, with streams of yellow streetlights leading off in defiantly long and endless lines, or the blush of morning settling across vast flat oceans. Let the sights lull you into a vacancy of mind that's a reasonable substitute for sleep. Enjoy the novelty of having the time to let your thoughts wander. Reflect on the wonder of being 10,000 metres up in the air.

To help you sleep, consider taking a small herb pillow, or the Jurlique product 'Travel Blend'. Melatonin is a natural hormone that induces sleep and is said to help reduce jet lag – ask your doctor or pharmacist about this. There are other drugs on the market, but know their effect on you before you fly – you don't want to arrive at your destination so groggy you don't know what to do or where you are. (There are tips for avoiding jet lag, and deep vein thrombosis, in Chapter 9.)

The mantra is always to avoid alcohol on long flights, and while avoiding excessive consumption is sensible, a glass of wine to wash down the airline food is an important part of creating the mood of the start of the journey for me. The food might be pretty ordinary, although really, surprisingly palatable given the logistics. Moments of simple pleasure can be found in the most mundane things. It's about a positive outlook. The cool glass of water in the middle of the night, the hot towel before breakfast is served, the aroma of bread rolls heating – they're not exciting moments, but they do represent the small symbols of travel, and can be celebrated as such.

TRAVEL TIP
Tips for surviving the flight:
- if possible, book a flight that arrives at night, so you can go straight to bed
- dress comfortably
- take a good book, crossword puzzles etc
- set yourself up in your seat with all that you'll need during the flight (which isn't much)
- if you normally wear contact lenses, swap them for a pair of glasses for the flight because your eyes dry out in the plane's atmosphere
- don't drink too much alcohol, but do allow yourself a celebratory tipple
- do drink lots of water (take your own water bottle on board – fill it once you've gone through the security check)
- avoid coffee, which is very dehydrating, and carbonated drinks that can make you feel uncomfortable
- remember that food is difficult to digest at high altitude, so don't overeat
- open your milk and salad dressing portions with great care and pointing away from you as the cabin pressure makes the contents squirt out
- be polite to the flight attendants – they will reward you with better service
- use the blanket and sleeping mask to replicate as closely as possible night time and bed
- don't get anxious if you can't sleep – use the time to daydream
- be grateful that those around you are also in an almost upright position – it does at least lessen the chance of snoring!
- be wary of starting a conversation with a fellow passenger if you don't want a chatterbox for twelve hours
- when the plane touches down at your destination, don't jump to your feet – there are still many long waits ahead of you

Problem passengers

Occasionally, you can find yourself next to a problem passenger. It may be that they are drunk, or annoying in some other way, or the passenger behind you is continually kicking your seat. Don't put up with the problem.

The best course of action is to walk to where the flight attendants are (usually the galley after a meal service) and ask to speak with the supervisor. Explain the situation and see if you can be moved to another seat. If the flight is full then ask that the supervisor have a word with the passenger. This enables the crew to monitor the person in case the problem increases, particularly if the aggressor is consuming alcohol. The crew need to be informed if they are to take precautionary measures before the problem gets out of control. Most if not all passengers calm down when spoken to by a uniform. If not, the cabin crewmember is legally allowed to take restraining action, something that you as the victim are not able to do.

The other problem you may encounter is sitting next to a very large person who is occupying part of your seat as well as their own. These days, most morbidly obese people are required to pay for two seats; however, exceptions occur and you are certainly entitled to a degree of comfort when travelling. Again, let the cabin crew know of your problem; they will always move you if they can. If the flight is full, your only other course of action is to later write to complain to the airline.

Stopovers, in transit and connections

Stopovers can be a welcome break in a long journey, a chance to mix up the cultural experiences and an opportunity to readjust your time clock. Or they can be a groggy drag that delays your arrival at your destination. For a stopover to be of any use in helping to ward off jet lag, you need a minimum of two nights – one night will only confuse your biological time clock even more.

The temperature differences between countries can be extreme, from a mere five degrees in Vienna to forty-five degrees in Dubai. The change can be debilitating, and you might need to pack extra clothes to cope with the extremes, thus increasing your luggage weight.

When considering stopovers, also think about the impact on the environment. Aircraft consume most of their fuel at take-off and landing, so limiting the number of stops in your journey helps to limit your contribution to greenhouse gas emissions.

In-transit time offers its own challenges. If you're flying to Europe, it's most likely that your in-transit stop is at the equivalent of the early hours of the morning, and you know, with some foreboding, that a twelve- to fourteen-hour leg lies ahead. Put your time in the airport to good use. You can duty-free shop, but keep in mind that the days of real savings are over. Being active while in transit will increase your chances of sleeping through the next long leg. So walk briskly, find a quiet corner to exercise, then relax over a herbal tea in a cafe. Some airports offer massages, gyms, showers, swimming pools, and hairdressers. Check out what is available and take advantage of what suits – *but watch the time*.

If you have a connecting flight at the end of your long haul, allow at least three hours between flights to give yourself some space in case of delays. If time is tight ask at your initial check-in to be checked in to the connecting flight.

TRAVEL TIP
When you check in at the start of your holiday, ask about checked-through luggage arrangements, so you know at what point you will need to collect your bags from a carousel. You won't need to collect them at your in-transit point. If you arrive at Heathrow, for example, and have a connecting flight from that airport, your luggage will normally be checked through. However, if you have a connecting flight from, say, Gatwick, you'll need to collect your luggage and take it on the shuttle to the next airport.

What to expect at airports
While some airports are definitely better than others (compare Schiphol airport in Amsterdam with Charles de Gaulle in France – how could the French do it so badly?), nearly all of them follow the same passenger processing pattern, from the layout of the airport between customs and the gate, to how and when passengers are checked in, called for flights and processed

through immigration, and baggage retrieval. Following is a run-down of the process at most international airports.

When you arrive at the airport for your flight:
- luggage is screened on entering some airports (although this doesn't happen in Australia)
- check in and receive a boarding pass with departure details, including the flight number, gate number and boarding time. Your checked luggage goes through screening activity behind the scenes
- proceed either to security screening or passport control. This varies from airport to airport, but as LAGs checks (Liquids, Aerosols and Gels – restricted or banned substances) become standard, it's seen as more practical to have screening first, so that LAGs problems can be rectified before passport control
- go to the nominated gate for your flight
- in Australia, international transit passengers move from arrivals to departures without going through passport control but they are re-screened to ensure their carry-on luggage complies with Australian standards. At other airports where arriving and departing passengers are mixed (and therefore screened passengers can exchange items with arriving passengers), they are re-screened at their new gate

When you arrive at your destination:
- pass through passport control, at which time your arrivals/declaration form will also be checked (the form is either handed out by cabin crew, or available at the airport as you approach the passport queue)
- proceed to the baggage carousel marked with your flight number and collect your luggage (in Australia, and now also in some other countries, your luggage will be sniffed by a dog in an official coat. These mild-looking creatures can get quite excited about the bag you used for food shopping)
- customs is the final check – some countries have a green line for 'nothing to declare' but in Australia, everyone is screened as part of quarantine protection

Beyond these functional issues, airports differ in the services they provide, the number of terminals (usually connected by light rail or shuttle bus services), the public transport connections available, and the security measures in place. Once again, the internet is invaluable as most airports have comprehensive sites that list their services and facilities.

TRAVEL TIP
- Use airport websites to check real-time flight information, to track flight arrival and departure times, delays and cancellations. There's usually a link from here directly to the airline's website for more information.
- Airport websites are also a good information source for finding out which carriers fly in and out. This is especially helpful when researching low-cost or domestic flights.

Large international airports are a world unto themselves, providing much more than just duty-free shopping. Their websites will include the following information, among other things:
- current passenger and security information
- transport to and from the airport
- airport map, especially showing adjacent railway stations, coach and shuttle bus stops, taxi ranks etc
- IT services: web kiosks, wireless access points, dial-up access points
- ATMs and foreign exchange bureaus
- cigarette-smoking stations
- chapels, mosques etc
- service stations to fill up your hire car before returning it to the depot
- luggage-wrapping service (if using, allow extra time before your flight departs)
- cafes, snack bars
- transit hotels
- medical services and pharmacies
- souvenir and bookshops
- showers
- massage and spa centres
- gym, swimming pool

You can print out relevant airport layout maps so that you can easily make your way from the arrivals area to the airport shuttle bus or train station, looking as though you've done it a thousand times before. Such knowledge is a terrific boost to travel confidence.

Transfers

You will have noticed people at airports holding aloft a card with a person's name on it, either before or after immigration control. These people are performing a service known as a 'transfer'. Normally booked through your travel agent, the guide will take you through the airport processes and help you with your luggage, getting money from an exchange or an ATM, and will have transport waiting to take you to your accommodation. It's a valuable service if you are not familiar with flying, or not confident, or if jet lag affects you so badly that you always feel disoriented upon arrival.

Short, cheap hops

Low-cost airlines have changed the nature of travelling between major cities, especially in western Europe, but along with the many benefits there are also some things to be aware of.

One of the reasons carriers can offer budget flights is that they use the airline portal as a means of selling a whole host of related tourism products such as accommodation, car hire or travel insurance. But also, instead of using main airports, they normally fly in and out of old air force bases, so their landing fees are much lower. Because of this, you need to carefully check the location of the airports you'll be using. Beware of the use of generic terms, such as Frankfurt, when the airport may in fact be at Hahn, nearly 200 kilometres away.

> **WEB SEARCH**
> For all low-cost carriers try **www.flycheapo.com**; two that fly to many destinations are **www.easyjet.com** and **www.ryanair.com**

CHECKLIST

- Where is the airport?
- Can you get to it easily?
- What is the luggage allowance? Some cheap flights do not allow luggage (for day business trips), or they may allow a maximum weight less than the twenty kilograms permitted by the long-haul carriers
- What is the excess baggage charge? It just might make the flight too expensive
- What are the add-on charges? Most charge extra for airport tax, credit card payment and luggage
- The tickets are usually non-refundable and sometimes non-changeable

TRAVEL TIP

Check the airport location. For example:
- London is unlikely to be Heathrow or Gatwick, but Stansted or Luton. If you are hoping for a connecting flight at Heathrow, Stansted is an hour-and-a-half coach trip away; it's nearly three hours from Gatwick.
- For Milan, the airport is Orio al Serio, and to get there you need to take a one-hour train ride from Milan central to Bergamo, then a connecting ten-minute train trip to the airport
- For Oslo, the airport is at Torp, and for some flights there is only one bus that leaves Oslo Central

Having said this, the low-cost airlines give you tremendous opportunity to find your way cheaply around Europe.

CHECKLIST

Here is a step-by-step guide to booking cheap flights:

- find out who flies where – on airport websites or **flycheapo.com**, or go to the destination maps on individual low-cost carrier sites. Do this early, as it might determine where your travels take you
- on the airline destination maps, click on a city and see what other cities it connects to (some hubs offer many more destinations than others)

- ❑ look at the name of the airport, for example Stansted airport for London
- ❑ go to the airport's website and make sure you can get to and from the airport within time constraints and transport availability
- ❑ check the cost of travelling to and from the airport, and factor this in to the overall fare
- ❑ check across as broad a range of dates as possible, as the fares can vary enormously and you'll occasionally be lucky enough to find one for 0.01 euros! (plus charges, of course)
- ❑ check the luggage allowance, luggage cost (it might be any luggage that goes into the hold) and excess-luggage rates
- ❑ go through the steps up to the point of purchase to see what the total cost is going to be
- ❑ be absolutely sure that you are ready to book, having the right dates and times for the flight
- ❑ book the flight/s
- ❑ print out and save the e-ticket and receipt, and file safely with your other travel documents

How safe is that plane?

There's no doubt: air travel is incredibly safe. Even so, one can't avoid that tremor of anxiety as the plane rushes down the runway, and we leave behind – far down there on the ground – all control over our own fate, until the bump of touchdown at our destination. In fact, it's all so totally out of our control, we might as well sit back and enjoy the ride.

Not so, perhaps, with some of the lesser-known airlines of the world – countries that have their own national airlines along with severe current account deficits, or companies with shady business backgrounds. You can check the reliability and record of airlines on the website of the International Civil Aviation Organisation. They have a section headed 'Global Aviation Safety Roadmap' where they list aircraft (and their operators) considered not to be airworthy.

> **WEB SEARCH**
> To check aircraft safety: www.casa.gov.au (in Australia) or www.icao.int (elsewhere)

TRAIN AND COACH TRAVEL

Choosing not to have a car can be wonderfully liberating, not to mention good for the environment. Trains and coaches take you into the heart of big cities without the stress of following unfamiliar street maps and searching for a car park.

Travelling by train

For all their efficiency and function, airports remain sterile places where passengers wander around in unforgiving bright light, removed from the real action that happens in restricted zones beyond the glass windows. Compare this with the atmosphere of a large central railway station. The steam and soot might be gone, but the romance lingers in the noise of trains shunting in and out. There's immediacy to the bustle and sense of departure because so many passengers are local residents going about their daily business.

Many of the big railway stations of Europe are great cavernous halls with massive spans of steel and filigree that recall an earlier age. The stations were built when rail ruled, and trains became the trigger for mass tourism. The destination boards click over, announcing the places one could so easily go: Geneva, Paris, Budapest, Antwerp. It's enticing to imagine dropping all plans and taking that train – right now – to Berlin.

Perhaps because long-distance train travel is so foreign to many Australians, it is a novel and relaxing way to travel in Europe. Economies of scale guarantee good trains: the sheer volume of passengers in Europe allows governments to invest in modern, fast and highly efficient services. Very fast trains are common in many European countries, and when you're on a budget, second-class travel is more than adequate.

Train travel can be much quicker than short-leg flights when travelling short distances. For example, Eurostar can take you from city-centre London to city-centre Paris in two and a half hours, with only a half-hour check-in, and passport and document checks on board. Plus, there's the space and freedom to walk up and down the aisles, the passing view of the countryside, the pleasure of eating at a table in the dining car, and the excitement of the under-channel tunnel. And the train trip is ten times less polluting than the equivalent flight.

Before the fast train was introduced for the British leg of Eurostar, the train wound through British towns at a tedious pace, and announcements were given in English first (with a strong French accent), then in French. On one train trip, as we approached the tunnel, the train gathered speed and we rocketed out into French territory and raced through the countryside into Paris. At some point while under the English Channel, English language was dropped and the announcements came thereafter in French only.

Tickets such as Eurail and Britrail, purchased with a predetermined number of days of travel, are economical and an easy way to travel between cities. There are usually discounts when two people are travelling together, and for seniors.

TRAVEL TIP
Be alert at large, crowded railway stations – they are a haven for pickpockets.

WEB SEARCH
For a one-stop site on train travel information in the UK and Europe, see **www.seat61.com**
When purchasing rail tickets in Australia: **www.railplus.com.au**

TRAVEL TIP
- plan your itinerary and work out how many days of train travel you will need so that you don't exceed your pass, or purchase more days than necessary
- consider sleepers – on the good European services the cabins are comfortable, the trip a great experience, and you can save on a night's accommodation elsewhere

In Norway, we travelled everywhere by train. The landscape is so breathtakingly beautiful and the train allowed us the time to take it in. The distances are enormous: we travelled in a sleeper from Roros to Bodo on a trip that took thirteen hours, north along the spine of Norway. It was rugged land, almost devoid of houses and farms. Forest, and more forest; water and more water. Our sleeping cabin had thick doonas and crisp white linen, and the buffet car served great food and hot chocolate.

On the return trip heading south, from Bodo to Trondheim, the train was a sprinter. There was no buffet car, but we stopped at small frontier-like stations and everyone climbed out onto the platform for a cigarette or to buy coffee. For meals, the conductor phoned orders through to be collected at the next station. During the journey, the train slowed and the immaculate purple-waist-coated train conductor announced that we were crossing the Arctic Circle, the invisible ring that circles the globe and marks the start of the land of the midnight sun. Beyond this point the sun does not rise on the winter solstice or set on the summer solstice. Reindeer raised their heads and watched us pass.

It's easy to work out train routes using each country's train services' website, or use the brilliant website The Man in Seat 61 (**www.seat61.com**) to find links to rail services throughout the world (it also gives figures comparing emission loads of flights compared with train travel). Most rail websites will give you times and distances between stations, detailed timetables, prices, maps, personalised routes with connections, and online bookings. You need all of this information (except the costs) if you're using a universal pass such as Eurail, so you know where and when to catch your train and make changes, and so you can tell your accommodation provider when you expect to arrive.

Then it's a matter of sitting back and enjoying the journey. Don't forget to pack a picnic lunch, as the buffet prices are usually pretty steep.

Seat reservations

There's usually no need to book a reserved seat out of season, but in peak times reservations remove the horror of having to lug your suitcases through twenty carriages looking for a vacant seat.

As well as knowing you have a guaranteed seat, you will know where to stand on the station (in most places), as the platform is marked with the carriage numbers that correspond with how the carriages pull into the station.

France and Italy are the two countries in which you might consider reserving seats even out of season, as they deal with such huge volumes of passengers throughout the year. Having a pass doesn't guarantee you a seat. Some of the high speed trains allocate a set number of seats for pass holders and if they've all been reserved you won't be able to travel on that train.

You can reserve a seat sixty days from your date of travel; on Eurostar you can reserve 120 days prior. Except for Eurostar, you can also reserve seats at any railway station in Europe as you go.

TRAVEL TIP

Some things to keep in mind when travelling by train:

- there are a range of different rail passes available; search for the one that best meets your needs
- do a crosscheck with prices on the individual rail services for the trips you plan to ensure that a railpass is the best value
- carefully calculate how many days of travel you need to purchase
- remember that a 'day' is midnight to midnight
- when travelling overnight, if you board after 7 p.m. you only use one day on your pass (recorded as your arrival day), unless you need to change trains before midnight, in which case you will be using two days
- before you use your rail pass for the first time, have it validated at the train station before you board the train. You'll need your passport to do this. After this initial validation, you just need to fill in the date you travel each time, and present your ticket and passport to the conductor for stamping
- most tickets are for non-smoking cabins (and most European trains are non-smoking) but check if this is important to you
- plan your travel to avoid back-tracking wherever possible, so you don't waste money and time
- you'll need to organise and pay extra for seat reservations and sleepers
- seat reservations may be necessary – you can arrange these before leaving home (online), or while travelling

- European trains are very prompt and only wait at stations for a few moments, so be ready with your luggage to board or to disembark as soon as the train stops
- most European trains are outstanding, and a second-class ticket will give you sufficient comfort and space
- many cities have multiple train stations – check carefully where you need to go for your train
- there are different timetables for weekday and weekends/public holidays

On intercity trains in Germany, at every seat there is a daily printout of timetables and connections and, with typical German precision, the trains are very fast (up to 280 kilometres per hour), state of the art, spotless and faultlessly prompt. Once, with a flight to catch, we felt very anxious that we had only a two-minute gap between connecting trains, but the conductor assured us that this would not be a problem. Our first train arrived on time to the minute; our second train was a few steps across the platform and departed exactly on time.

Coach travel

Travelling by bus across large distances is economical, if not always time-efficient. If you want to explore small, out-of-the-way villages, buses can be a good option. While some companies specialise in coach travel for backpackers (hop-on, hop-off services), others operate in much the same way as Eurail. Eurolines is a network of coach companies that travel to 500 destinations; you can buy a Eurolines pass online. It's necessary to pre-book your first journey, and after that you can book as you travel. In Britain, National Express offers a similar service, known as Go By Coach.

> **WEB SEARCH**
> For information and tickets for coaches through Europe:
> www.eurolines.com and
> www.nationalexpress.com

ON THE ROAD
Car hire
Car hire comes into its own if you want to travel through regional areas and to out-of-the-way places. Your own vehicle will give you the freedom to leave the main highways and start to explore the back roads and small villages in regional areas. You'll never find a gem on an autobahn, but a quiet lane might reveal the highlight of your holiday.

There's nothing special about selecting a car – all the types and sizes are known the world over, although the terms and small-print costs can vary tremendously. The price you actually pay is often much more than the advertised price because of all the add-ons. Fuel is much more expensive in Britain and Europe, so hire a vehicle with a small engine, and go for diesel if possible.

If you are planning to drive to out-of-the-way places, it pays to use a reputable, widely based car-hire company that will be available to help you if you have problems. There are some very good websites that allow you to search for the best option across all available car-hire companies, but it's worth doing a crosscheck with individual company websites.

TRAVEL TIP
- give yourself time to recover from jet lag before driving (eg a couple of days in a city using public transport)
- global brands (Hertz, Avis, Europcar) might be slightly more expensive, but the car will be less than two years old, and the terms should include free roadside service
- usually, the earlier you book, the cheaper the rate
- it normally costs more to pick up a hire car at the airport than downtown; compare the cost with taking an airport bus to town for car collection
- check the location of where you are to pick up the car; besides the airport, car-hire companies are often tucked away in back streets
- diesel is much more economical than petrol, and many European cars use this fuel
- consider a hybrid car (petrol/electric) to save on fuel and emissions
- keep in mind the size of your luggage when selecting a vehicle

- don't go too small or too cheap, as you'll probably be spending many hours driving
- ask for a vehicle equipped with GPS, which is a fantastic tool when you don't know a region – simply key in your next accommodation address and keep following the instructions until the voice tells you, 'You have arrived'
- it's much cheaper to opt for returning the car with a full tank of fuel, and airports have service stations close by to make this easy
- care for the car; it may not be yours, but that doesn't give you the right to mistreat it or drive poorly
- hire cars often don't automatically come with good maps, but if you ask, the company will nearly always give you one
- the car-hire company sticker on the car is a giveaway that you're a tourist – don't leave anything valuable in the car

CHECKLIST

Check the car-hire terms and conditions for the following:

- ❑ insurance – what does it include? (also check your travel insurance; it could be that you are already covered for car-hire insurance)
- ❑ excess on claims
- ❑ limits to use, such as no driving on unsealed roads, not taking the car on ferries (if you break the terms you'll void your insurance)
- ❑ one-way relocation cost
- ❑ limit of kilometres per day or per period of hire
- ❑ time for return of the car – if you're late you'll be charged an extra day
- ❑ whether you have to pay more if nominating a second driver
- ❑ conditions applying to age of driver
- ❑ age of car
- ❑ roadside service agreement
- ❑ surcharge for airport pick-up
- ❑ any other 'hidden' extra costs

> **WEB SEARCH**
> For car-hire comparisons: www.travelsupermarket.com (among many)

When you take delivery of the car, look over it carefully, in the presence of the attendant, for any damage for which you may later be blamed. Ask for two sets of keys: the loss of keys can cause significant delays if you don't have a backup.

Car leasing

If you are travelling for more than a month, car leasing may be a cheaper option. In Europe, both Citroen and Peugeot offer leasing arrangements, for which there are positives and negatives:
- you can lease the car tax free
- you have unlimited kilometres
- you may be responsible for arranging the first service (you'll need to have driven 10,000 kilometres)
- check that you can go outside the country in which you leased the car

> **WEB SEARCH**
> For car leasing: www.citroen.com.au/driveeurope or www.peugeot.com.au

Left-hand drive

Remember that in many countries you'll be driving on the right-hand side of the road. Once you've taught yourself to get into the left side of the car to drive, it's important to also train yourself to remember your position on the road: the driver always sits on the side of the car that is nearest to the centre line. Keep alert; when you need to react quickly your first instincts may be wrong.

Perhaps more alarming than left-hand drive is the speed on the autobahns. Speeds of up to 200 kilometres per hour are quite normal, but can be disconcerting when you're used to Australian highways. You need to take great caution, and be

CAR-HIRE COMPARISON

Company name		
Website address		
Type of car		
Age of car		
Size of engine		
No. of people		
Sedan/wagon/hatchback		
Manual/automatic		
Petrol/diesel		
Km per day allowance		
Insurance		
Excess on claims		
One-way relaocation cost		
Airport pick-up surcharge		
Pick-up depot location		
Drop-off depot location		
Pick-up/drop-off times		
Roadside service		
2nd driver cost		
GPS fitted		
Airconditioning		
Right to travel beyond country of pick-up		
Unsealed roads okay? (if applicable)		
Ferry trips okay? (if applicable)		
Other costs		
Other features		
Driver's age excess		

aware of the road rules and protocols. You can study these in advance on the website nationalcar.co.uk/drivesafe/english. Allow extra time for travelling, despite the speeds, as car accidents are common and can block highways for hours.

> **WEB SEARCH**
> See the website **www.nationalcar.co.uk/drivesafe/english** for country-by-country road rules
> **www.viamichelin.com** is an invaluable source of information for maps, driving distances and times, toll charges, route plans, and GPS navigation aids and map updates

Motorhomes

One of the main attractions of using a motorhome as your mode of transport is that once you've unpacked, you can keep on moving about without bringing out the suitcases time and again. They're self-contained and usually very comfortable, and reasonably easy to manoeuvre.

In Northern Europe and the UK, motorhomes are really only an option in the summer months, and they're more appropriate in some countries than others, depending on the number and spread of camping sites. Because of their size, and because of a dearth of camping grounds within large cities, motorhomes are best used for open-road travel. In those cities that do have camping grounds, they are often far from the city centre.

> **WEB SEARCH**
> Visit **www.campingcardinternational.com** for a comprehensive list of campsites in Europe

You can purchase a Camping Card International (CCI) from your state automobile association, which gives you a welcome at campsites (some European camping grounds will not admit non-holders) and discounts at some campsites. It also includes third-party insurance against compensation for bodily injury to third parties, and/or damage to property resulting from any accident that occurs while camping. The documentation comes with a directory of campsites.

When selecting a motorhome, check carefully to see what the price does and does not include, such as the first tank of fuel, gas, cooking equipment or bedding; also check all the issues that apply to car hire.

International Driving Permits

An International Driving Permit (IDP) is required in some countries, and in Australia the automobile associations are charged with the task of issuing these permits. Go to the website of your state automobile association, such as the RACV in Victoria, where you will find the following:
- which countries require you to have an IDP
- which side of the road is used in each country
- how to apply for a permit
- validity – usually twelve months
- what other documents you need to support your IDP
- how they work
- what they cost

An IDP is a United Nations officially sanctioned document, so it can be used as another form of identity. This can be handy – you can leave your passport tucked away safely and use the IDP for cashing traveller's cheques and on other occasions when you need to prove your identity.

> **WEB SEARCH**
> Your state automobile association can help you with Camping Cards International and IDPs:
> New South Wales: www.mynrma.com.au
> Northern Territory: www.aant.com.au
> Queensland: www.racq.com.au
> South Australia: www.raa.net
> Tasmania: www.ract.com.au
> Victoria: www.racv.com.au
> Western Australia: www.rac.com.au

TAKE TO THE WATER

Mixing up your modes of travel can add colour to your journey. Boat travel allows you to view a place from a surprisingly different angle. As well as offering lots of information about train travel, The Man in Seat 61 website (**www.seat61.com**) also gives a list of all the ferry services in the UK and Europe. Another good site is **www.aferry.to**, which provides information on connections for all over Europe. Using these sites, you could put together an itinerary travelling across Britain and Europe without ever needing a car or flight. Ferries offer routes that can enliven an otherwise conventional itinerary: Sweden to Estonia, Croatia to Italy, England to Spain, Germany to Finland, Greece to Cyprus, along the Norwegian coast, France to Morocco … You'll need to do more research to find out what's available and how to put it all together, but you can end up with a unique, memorable experience.

> **WEB SEARCH**
> Ferry information can be found at **www.seat61.com** and **www.aferry.to**

Ferries are great because you can usually take your hire car with you, but be careful to always book with reputable ferry companies. If you think a vessel looks unseaworthy or overcrowded, don't travel on it.

For a touch more adventure, why not swap your land legs for a week on a charter boat. I'm biased, having been in the charter boat industry for over twenty years, but I still can't imagine anything more wonderfully relaxing than spending time on a boat. There's something magical about casting off – you move into a different environment, and the everyday disappears. Your sailing can take you into the limitless blue of the Aegean, or from Sicily into the Mediterranean, or to the thousand islands along the Dalmatian coast. You'll get to see exotic places from a different perspective; the sense of arrival at a port has a charm all of its own. Moor at a small harbour town and have your senses

AIR AND GROUND: GETTING AROUND 73

assaulted by the noise of harbour activity, the calls of foreign tongues, and the smells from cafes cooking the day's catch. You can swap salty stories with fellow sailors who hail from all corners of the earth. And when you want to escape civilisation, your means is right there – a tiller and a breeze await you.

TRAVEL TIP
- with a skippered charter you do no more than lie on the deck and soak up the sun
- if you can't sail, take a pre-charter sailing course (ask for details at your local yacht club)
- if you can sail, why would you miss the opportunity to practise your skills in the most exotic places on earth?

For really simple boating, take a canal barge in the Netherlands, France, Belgium, Italy, Germany or the UK. Nothing could be easier, meandering along gentle waterways, learning the tricks to lock operation, cycling off to the local bakery for baguettes, watching the rural countryside drift by, past windmills and tulips, grazing cattle and tiny villages, stopping where and when you please.

When you take a boating holiday, you unpack at the start, and travel in the most spectacular way, taking your accommodation with you.

And, of course, there are the large cruise ships, but they're perhaps not the domain for travellers seeking unprescribed experiences, as cruise liners ensure that everything is on board to capture passengers' attention and dollars. They're a good option for the less mobile and the very social, but their style and purpose puts them outside the scope of this book. Cruise travel is best researched with a travel agent.

WEB SEARCH
for boat charters (skippered and bareboat) in Europe:
www.marinerboating.com.au
for canal boats: **www.canalboatholidays.com**

EXPLORING LOCALLY

Once you've arrived at your destination it's time to slow down the pace and movement to local public transport and walking. Feet are good for shorter distances. In fact, feet are fantastic. They'll take you at a human pace into the back alleys and through suburban streets, they'll allow you to stop for a coffee, and start moving again whenever you want. They're flexible, free and environmentally friendly. You just need a good pair of walkers, a small backpack and a map.

Local buses, trams and trains within a city are much easier than bothering with a car, and using these services will make you feel like a local as you line up in the morning with the city's residents going off to work. After a few days, someone might even acknowledge you with a small smile – an example of inclusion that will make you feel good all day.

It can be a headache trying to work out how to pay for public transport tickets – every country, every city, seems to have its own methods, sometimes completely hidden from visitors. The best way to find out is to ask at the local tourist information office. They often sell city passes for a set number of days that give you unlimited public transport use, plus free entry to museums, and discounts at a range of venues, shops and restaurants. You can check this out in advance by going to the tourism information office website to see what they offer.

In those watery cities with canals and islands, travelling by ferry, vaporetti or canal boat is usually efficient and adds to the flavour of your experience, especially if it's not your normal public transport mode. Funicular railways or tramways and chairlifts are in the same category.

TRAVELLING GREEN

You only have to arrive at an airport and breathe in the aviation fuel fumes to be reminded that travel comes at a significant cost to the environment. A return flight to Europe will create greenhouse gas emissions equivalent to about two years of car use. Air travel currently contributes about 2 per cent of global warming impact, and this is set to rise by more than 250 per cent in the next fifty years. Unless you decide that the environmental cost is too great to fly (and this is an admirable position to take), there are other ways to ease the burden of your travels.

The easiest approach is to purchase carbon offsets, that is, to pay for your CO_2 load on the environment to a company that will use the money on projects such as renewable energy, energy efficiency and forest restoration. There are any number of companies that allow you to purchase emission offsets online. For example, with Climate Care (a UK company), you simply enter in the flights you will be taking (for example, Melbourne to Rome and return, Rome to Madrid, one way), and the approximate kilometres you think you will drive, and the site will calculate the offsets you need to purchase. Then you go to 'checkout' and make your purchase.

> **WEB SEARCH**
> You can purchase emissions offsets on a number of sites. Calculations vary, as do the ways your money is used to save the environment.
> www.elementree.com.au
> www.carbonneutral.com.au
> www.easybeinggreen.com.au
> www.co2australia.com.au
> www.climatecare.org
> www.greenfleet.com.au
> www.climatefriendly.com

Other green travelling ideas to keep in mind:
- walk wherever possible – it will help to keep you fit, compensate for the cake at morning tea, slow down your pace of travel, and take a load off the environment
- get on a bike. Some cities offer bicycles as a way of getting around – another good green option
- if hiring a car, choose one that is energy efficient, or a hybrid
- drive more slowly to reduce fuel consumption
- choose public transport rather than car hire or taxis

- go sailing – it's about as green as travel and accommodation can get
- plan for a minimum number of stopovers, as it's take-offs and landings that use the most fuel
- think twice before booking a cheap, short flight if train travel is available
- fly less frequently and stay longer when you do travel

4

HOMES AWAY FROM HOME

*A journey is best measured in friends,
rather than miles.*

Tim Cahill

- On the hunt
- Why book in advance?
- How many pillows?
- Spoilt for choice
- All the comforts of home
- Moments of serendipity
- Varying the experience
- Power up
- Guests and hosts
- Staying green

ON THE HUNT

The internet is a wonderful travel-planning tool. It can give you information about destinations, train timetables, out of the way B&Bs – it's all there at your fingertips. But there are some snags to be wary of as you start to plan the details of your holiday.

First, there's the sheer volume of information. Only about 20 per cent of web content is ever accessed. Go to Google and enter a general term like 'London accommodation' and you'll get over 30 million links. No-one is ever going to search through all those millions of pages – the majority of users rarely go past the first page of links. And most of the pages will have little or nothing to do with accommodation in London.

Search engines such as Google do attempt to prioritise in order of relevance: the order in which the links appear is known as PageRank on Google. However, the order is not only about relevance, but also about the number of hits a site gets. Sites can get a lot of hits because they appear on page one, and they appear on page one because they get a lot of hits.

Many sites are ranked highly because they are, in reality, far more general than just about 'London accommodation'. The top listings are likely to be websites that represent accommodation providers all over the world. There's nothing wrong with this, but small businesses cannot compete with their volume of traffic, so will never bump them off the first page. To find individual businesses you have to go a way down the list of links.

On the one hand, Google is terrifically convenient and fast; on the other, you need to approach the results of your search with some alertness, if not scepticism. We can easily fall into the trap of thinking that PageRank helps to give us the most suitable sites, but it's often not the case.

There are any number of websites now that offer accommodation at reduced rates: **www.lastminute.com**, **www.ratestogo.com** and **www.wotif.com** to name but a few. Most give you a window of a couple of weeks for advance bookings. They're good to use if you're happy to book accommodation as you go, and if your preference is for hotels. But they won't help much with special, unusual and out of the way places. Be sure to check what currency is being quoted on the site.

How do you become a more discriminating internet user?
- look for official websites – those of the country or the city you want to search. Do this by using the search words (in inverted commas) 'official visitor guide', eg 'Spain official visitor guide', or 'Prague official visitor guide'. These sites will generally give you the broadest and least biased information about accommodation and other tourism information. They also usually provide links to individual business operators' websites so you can deal direct
- use succinct keywords and the range of words that best

suits your search; for example, rather than 'London accommodation', try 'London budget self-contained accommodation'
- look at the actual website address, in green type at the bottom of the Google listing. Does it look like what you need? For example, if you search by business name, the business's website might be sixth or seventh on the page. The sites that come up first may be booking agents, or have some loose connection with the business
- be prepared to search beyond page one, through at least the first six pages if you can be bothered, or at least until you start to hit less relevant sites
- try using Google's advanced search features. This gives you options for selecting *all* words to be searched, or an exact phrase, or a search that excludes specific words
- try other search engines beyond Google; for example, on Gigablast you can narrow your search to 'Travel', and when you enter a destination, it will give you all the relevant tourism options (Gigabits)
- approach search engines as tools that require attention and time, rather than seeing them as convenient and easy

TRAVEL TIP
To find a small, niche business:
- start with the official website of the country you're visiting
- select the region/s within the country you wish to visit
- select the accommodation section (usually searchable by type, location and price)
- click through to the individual websites, where available, and contact directly

Once you've found a range of accommodation providers that look suitable, how will you determine the professionalism, reliability and integrity of these operators? A Hilton is a Hilton, but how do you work out if the cosy B&B you've found on the internet exists, and will deliver what it promises?

The short answer is, there's no real foolproof way, and if this concerns you, you're better to stick to either booking with major

chains or using the services of a travel agent. However, there are some reliable indicators. Look for the following:
- the quality of the website – if it's been thrown together with out-of-focus images and poor copy, it might be a reflection of how the business is run
- the language – if it's full of instructions about what you're not allowed to do, it's a fair bet customer service isn't their strength
- the inclusion of features and prices (and what the rate includes)
- a variety of images – study the photos carefully, beyond the nicely folded towel on the bed. Is there a broad range of photos, or just the one carefully cropped scene?
- the inclusion of a map or details of location
- mention of independent accreditation, tourism awards, or other industry accolades or certificates
- documented terms and conditions, including payment and cancellation

TRAVEL TIP
When sending an email, ask the following questions:
- is the property available on the dates you require?
- what is the total price? In what currency?
- what does the price include?
- what are the payment terms?
- what form of receipt or voucher is issued?
- what are the check-in and check-out times?
- how do you get to the property from the airport, train station, by car etc?
- if relevant, where do you collect the key?
- how far is the property from the CBD (or whatever the reason for selecting the location)?
- any special request you might have – parking space, a ground-floor room, special dietary needs, early check-in or late check-out etc

Send an email and gauge the response. Is it quick? Is it professional? Does it answer all the questions you asked? Is it friendly rather than off-hand? Also keep in mind that some countries are more web-savvy than others. For example, I can send emails to twenty accommodation businesses in Ireland requesting information and maybe get three responses. I can send twenty to Germany and get twenty responses. Sometimes you just have to persevere.

In some countries, it's routine practice for an operator to ask for advance payment. This always makes me feel more comfortable because the operator is absolutely obliged to honour the booking. And it gives me a greater sense of their professionalism. If you're paying by credit card and the operator doesn't have a secure system, send your credit card number and details divided over two or three emails.

> **WEB SEARCH**
> Use Google maps (**www.maps.google.com**) to locate accommodation and print out street maps to take with you

WHY BOOK IN ADVANCE?

You arrive at your destination late in the afternoon, tired from your travels and anxious for a place to dump your bags. You head straight to the tourism information centre – always a good source for accommodation availability. But this time, there's a long queue of seriously disgruntled tourists in front of you. Unbeknown to them – and to you – Mick Jagger and his band have arrived in town for a one-night-only concert and every known bed has already been booked by fans. It happens; and in these days when cities use major events to drive their tourism, it is happening more and more frequently. This is just one reason to book in advance. You march smugly past the queue and buy your city transport card, then go straight to your waiting accommodation.

Many people think that advance accommodation bookings rob their travels of serendipity, but there are more things in favour of pre-planning than against. Here are a few more reasons to book in advance:
- you can search on the internet for small, out of the way places that you would never find if you waited until you arrived in a new city

- if you wait until you arrive, the places easiest to find, eg hotels, are rarely unique
- you can compare attributes and prices in advance. Unless you're prepared to trudge backwards and forwards between possible places to stay, you don't have the same opportunity to get the most for your dollar as you do when planning in advance
- if you find something special (or friends tell you of the best apartment in Innsbruck) and don't book it, there's every chance it will not be available when you arrive
- your internet search might take you into an area you previously didn't consider or didn't know about, for example, staying at beautiful Cefalu instead of noisy Palermo and simply catching the train into the city centre
- you can waste a good half-day searching for suitable accommodation – with all the related stress and waste of precious holiday time
- the later in the day you arrive at a destination, the greater the anxiety and pressure to find something suitable and affordable
- if you arrive when the visitor information centre is closed, you can be really stumped
- accommodation in the suburbs, with access to good public transport, will be quieter and less expensive, but difficult to find if you haven't pre-booked
- it is still possible to find some amazing bargains on the internet, and you can find delightfully individual styles of accommodation

HOW MANY PILLOWS?

This is the question I ask myself when starting to plan an itinerary. What I mean is, how many different places do I want to stay at? How many different cities, how much travelling, how much packing and unpacking? Consider that the time spent in the car, on the train, in flight, is time lost rubbing shoulders with the locals and experiencing difference. Travelling is enormously time-consuming, and it does take a toll – if your holiday is to be relaxing as well as rewarding, you don't want to spoil it with rushing from place to place.

The longer you stay in any one place, the more you can crawl under its skin, getting to know the streets, the good cafes, the bus timetables – all the small things that can make you feel, just for a little while, that you're one of the locals, and help you to really learn about the culture and customs.

Slow travel is the most rewarding. In a four- or five-week trip, I'd aim for no more than four or five pillows. That probably means staying for at least seven nights in any one place, to get to know the sights, the sounds and ways of life. I love the feeling of moving into a small apartment in a city, or holiday house in the country, unpacking my bags, and settling in to the art of belonging.

SPOILT FOR CHOICE

Accommodation varies enormously, from luxury five-star hotels to grubby one-room *pensionnes*. Unfortunately, price isn't always a good indicator, especially towards the bottom end of the range. In a big city, or in a small town where there's limited choice, you can pay a lot of money for grunge. The worst accommodation we ever had was in a hotel in Port Louis in Brittany. It was the only accommodation in town, but even that was no excuse for the dark-brown shag-pile carpet that crept up the walls, the dripping shower in the corner of the room, and the toilet down the hall. Its one redeeming feature was not of its own making – from our window, we looked out onto a beautiful church steeple.

Bed and breakfasts

If you're travelling through many places, spending only a night or two at any one spot (lots of pillows!), B&Bs come into their own. They are more personal and individual than hotels, giving you a better insight into the authenticity of a place, but it is very much a case of 'buyer beware'.

Australia's standard of B&B accommodation is generally very high, with professional hosts and delicious breakfasts. But that's not the case in many countries. A friend of mine talks about 'death by doily' – those rooms where there are more floral patterns per square metre than cornflakes in a bowl. I think there might be a mathematical formula that shows that the number of floral patterns is inversely proportional to the level of professionalism.

If booking a B&B, look carefully and critically at the photos on the website. You'll also want to know the following:
- does the room have an ensuite or private bathroom? (Certainly, you don't want to share the owner's bathroom.) Is it a real bathroom, or a converted cupboard?
- is there a guest lounge room?
- can you use the garden?
- what is the breakfast menu? (Many English B&Bs claim exotic breakfast menus, but it's often just greasy, run-of-the-mill eggs and bacon
- do they offer dinner in-house?
- will they pack a picnic lunch for you?
- is there a safe place to park your car?

None of this, however, will save you from a fruitcake host. We once stayed in a B&B where the host was lifted straight out of *Fawlty Towers*. In the evening, we couldn't escape from his railing about communism and the state of the country; at breakfast he refused to talk to us.

There are some very reputable B&B guides, available by country or by city, but keep in mind that in most cases the B&B operator has paid to be in the guide.

> **WEB SEARCH**
> For an extensive list of B&Bs, see
> www.bedandbreakfastineurope.com

Guesthouses

Guesthouses can be a slightly safer option compared with B&Bs, as you're more removed from hosts and their personalities, but still have the sense of living within the local style. Many guesthouses provide breakfast, normally in the traditional style of the country: in Amsterdam there'll be piles of soft-boiled eggs keeping warm under padded cloths; in Greece, *trahana* (pasta) soup with soft fetta and wild honey. Some guesthouses offer communal kitchens, which help conserve the budget.

Many guesthouses are in older buildings, often with steep staircases and without lifts.

Hotels

Hotels are a good, safe, if unimaginative option if you are travelling every day. What we consider typically four-star accommodation, for example, will be fairly uniform across a broad range of hotels. However, in Europe it can be a pretty mixed bag – four-star in some countries is equivalent to about two-star here. The ICE hotels throughout Germany, always within a stone's throw of the central railway station, are particularly good value. Booking global brand hotels, or those that belong to a chain, is a safe option. Unless you've booked in advance, ask to see the room before you commit.

A hotel room will never feel like home. Their purpose, in part, is to offer a sense of security by being totally predictable. The bed goes here, the chair goes there, the bathroom in the corner. In Britain, like Australia, extras such as an iron and tea- and coffee-making facilities are usually standard, but don't expect these in most European hotels, especially the budget variety.

Some hotels will offer a small bar fridge, and some even a microwave oven. Check out these facilities when you book. But even if there are no options for meal preparation, that doesn't stop you buying a good bottle of red, some bread, salami and cheese, and feasting like a king in your room.

Hostels

Gradually the 'youth' is losing its hold in 'youth hostels' as this form of accommodation becomes more popular with older, budget-wise travellers, known as 'flashpackers'.

Flashpackers are anywhere from twenty to seventy years old. They are prepared to economise on accommodation, so as to have money to afford experiences and good food. They'll put up with roughing it, but not too much. While some backpacker hostels are still definitely for the young – with all the stereotypical attributes of grime, drugs, alcohol, loud music and rock-hard beds – many are providing a higher standard of accommodation.

You can find hostels that offer private rooms, some with ensuites. They also have communal areas such as lounge rooms and kitchens, which are good meeting places to talk to others about travel experiences and their 'must see' recommendations, or compare ways of life. Hostels can be found in city centres and regional areas, and are often on the local bus route or close to railway stations, making them easy to get to if you don't have a car.

The downside is that, as hostels get smarter, the rock-bottom prices are being replaced with something closer to the cost of a conventional budget hotel. But do some research – you might be pleasantly surprised.

Motorhomes, boats

These are discussed in more detail in Chapter 3. Motorhomes offer flexibility and freedom; boats offer a wide range of facilities and a chance to truly spread your wings. I think of these forms as 'tortoise travel', whereby you carry your home with you.

ALL THE COMFORTS OF HOME

My preference is for self-contained accommodation, partly for the space it offers, but more because when you stay in accommodation without cooking facilities, having to dine out for every meal quickly eats into your budget.

Within the term 'self-contained' you will find everything from a serviced hotel room with a microwave to a large holiday house with a swimming pool. Whatever your choice, check carefully as to what is included in the price.

We once booked an apartment in Paris – bedroom, kitchen, bathroom – only to find that the kitchen was bare. If we wanted plates, pots, cutlery, detergent or tea towels, they were all available, but at an extra cost. So ask some probing questions before you book.

Apartments

City-centre apartments are hard to beat in terms of location, space, and a range of handy facilities. You can settle into an apartment in quite a different way from settling into a hotel room – there's a sense of 'living' rather than 'staying'.

If you're staying in a city for more than a couple of days, it's lovely to have the feeling of home. Hotels seem to have a 'tip out into the streets' feel, where you are either on the go, seeing the sights, or in bed sleeping. However, an apartment will make you feel that you want to use the space as another experience of your holiday. A place to linger over breakfast, return for lunch, do the laundry, or stretch out on a couch to read on a wet afternoon.

When you stay in an apartment, you'll find yourself saying at the end of a hard day's sightseeing: 'Let's go home'. If your apartment is in the suburbs, you'll have a lovely sense of going home as you walk along gradually familiar streets, or know which train to catch. You can add some extra touches to make your stay even more homely: a bowl of fruit, a candle on the table for dinner, your books and maps on the coffee table, your shawl across the couch.

You can move the furniture around a little – bring the table to the window that overlooks the bustling cobbled lane – but do the cleaner the favour of always returning the furniture to its original position at the end of your stay.

Some apartments come with daily servicing, but in the budget range you're usually left to your own devices for the length of your stay.

Holiday houses

Individual and often great value for money, a holiday house is the best way of all to feel like you belong. They're wonderful if you're travelling with a group of friends, but even for two people, they can offer exceptional experiences, especially through small touches and personal decorating. They are a particularly good choice when staying in regional areas or small towns as they are often built in the local style, giving a greater sense of place.

A holiday house can also be a let-down if you're confronted with grubbiness and lack of equipment, so again, you need to do some serious research. There are many professional websites that invite holiday-house owners to list their properties, while preserving all the individual touches of an owner-manager at the house. However, ensuring consistent quality can be a problem. There are also sites where a manager is responsible for a portfolio of houses. The manager usually ensures that all the houses are maintained at a professional standard.

TRAVEL TIP
When searching for a holiday house, consider the following questions:
- How does the web-host company select properties, ie what is your assurance that the property exists and is of the standard portrayed?
- Does the website look professional?
- How many photos are there? Are there photos of each room?
- Can you pay with a credit card, or does the owner only accept cash?
- Are you asked for prepayment? If so, are the payment arrangements secure with the issue of a receipt? (Prepayment is usually a benefit, as you are entering into a confirmed arrangement that the property will definitely be held for your arrival.)
- Do you book with and pay the website manager, or do you click through to the individual property owner's website and deal direct?
- What are the arrangements for key collection and property inspection?
- Who do you contact if something goes wrong at the property?

WEB SEARCH
Some sites (out of hundreds) for holiday houses:
www.vrbo.com – lists holiday houses worldwide, considered to be largest website of its kind; rentals are directly with the house owner
www.sawdays.co.uk – Alistair Sawday's special places to stay; includes green places to stay plus B&B and self catering
www.i-escape.com – good site but more pricey
www.ownersdirect.co.uk – advertises villa and apartment rentals worldwide
See official tourism websites for more links

The best recommendations for holiday houses come from friends – those who have found a gem and are happy to share their knowledge. The other place to find out about holiday houses is in the travel accommodation listings in the back pages of lifestyle magazines.

CHECKLIST

To help you decide what you want, rank the following in order of what you think is most important to least important.

- Price – add here your per-night budget: $......... to $.........
- Walking distance to city centre
- Close to public transport
- Quiet street
- Busy city centre
- Non smoking
- Star rating
- Green/eco rating
- Size of bed (twin/queen/king)
- Separate kitchen
- Shower
- Bath
- Laundry facilities
- Separate lounge room
- TV, DVD, CD
- Internet connection
- Ground floor
- Upstairs
- Stairs or elevator
- Close to supermarket
- Owner/manager
- Outdoor area – garden, barbecue etc
- View of water
- View of city
- View of icon, eg Eiffel Tower
- Car parking
- Daily room servicing
- Other important attributes:

....

House swaps

This is a system of 'you stay in my house while I stay in yours', which means free accommodation almost anywhere in the world. The procedure is similar to that of internet dating – you find something that looks suitable and exchange emails directly with the owner to build up a feeling of whether the swap would work. If you can arrange a suitable house exchange, it means considerable savings; some owners also exchange car use. Such accommodation gives you a chance to live at a grassroots level in a community.

> **WEB SEARCH**
> There are many house-swap websites, including
> **www.homeexchange.com**,
> listing properties in over 100 countries

The problem with this system is that it can take a lot of organising, certainly more advance planning, and you need to find someone who wants your house at the same time as you want theirs. The burden is eased by the fact that many houses offered are second or holiday homes, giving more flexibility with dates.

MOMENTS OF SERENDIPITY

Just in case you think all pre-planning is too prescriptive, robbing you of unique, spontaneous experiences, let me tell you a story.

We booked accommodation in Northern Wales on one trip. We turned off the main road, leaving behind all those bungalows and caravan parks, and wound up a narrow country lane, past a scattering of working farms to find a comfortable two-storey traditional stone farmhouse set in a small garden. A blue shimmer to the west was the broad expanse of Cardigan Bay; to the north Mount Snowdon; and all around us rugged gorse-yellowed farmland.

The farmer who owned the house (he lived in a more modern equivalent further down the lane) was teaching his young border collie to round up sheep, and as we are suckers for dogs, we watched with pleasure. Afterwards, we had a good yarn about the price of wool and the effects of global warming. As he was leaving, the farmer asked if we'd like to go along to choir practice that evening, in the next village. Fred rolled his eyes, but I quickly accepted the invitation.

When we arrived at the local primary school, the farmer was waiting for us and he showed us to a couple of chairs especially put out for our benefit. The choir comprised about sixty men, between the ages of fifty and late eighties, all of whom spoke Welsh as their first language. The farmer's son was the conductor, and he explained to us that the choir was rehearsing Welsh hymns, which were new to them so it might not sound so appealing. We listened as the tenors practised their parts, the baritones, the basses. It sounded okay, but then the conductor put it all together – and it sounded magnificent. The most wonderful sounds were issuing from this group of Welsh farmers; it was intensely emotional to listen to them.

After an hour's practice, two women arrived with fresh milk and cakes, and laid out supper for the singers. Talking to the men, we quickly realised that this was no ordinary local choir. 'Australia?' they queried. 'Oh yes, we sang with the Sydney Philharmonia Choirs a couple of years back. This year, we toured Europe. Oh, and we won the National Eisteddford.' In this simple classroom, with strings of paper people and alphabet pictures, we were honoured to witness something very special.

No serendipity with pre-booked accommodation? Don't you believe it.

VARYING THE EXPERIENCE

If you've opted for a few pillows during your travels, try to vary the accommodation experience, and attempt to stay somewhere that seems representative of the place. Not kitsch, but perhaps an apartment block from the fifties, or a renovated farmhouse, or a guesthouse that has been operating for a century or more. The Paradores in Spain and Pousadas in Portugal offer unique accommodation in old monasteries, castles and stately homes, usually serving traditional food and often in spectacular settings.

ACCOMMODATION COMPARISON

Use one sheet per destination and compare the attributes of your short-listed accommodation choices.
Give rating: 1 poor, 5 excellent

DESTINATION:

Business name		
Street address		
Website address		
No. of nights		
Cost per night		
Form of payment		
Deposit required		
Distance from central site		
Proximity to public transport		
Proximity to supermarkets/shops		
Electricity/water included		
Linen/towels included		
No. of bedrooms		
Bathroom facilities		
Kitchen facilities		
Laundry facilities		
Breakfast included		
Ground floor/upstairs		
Daily servicing included		
Cleaning cost on departure		
Other services		

ACCOMMODATION DETAILS

Here is an example of a spreadsheet to allow you to keep track of your reservations, including dates, costs, inclusions. Download a copy of this spreadsheet from The Five Mile Press website.

TOWN	ACCOMMODATION	CHECK IN	CHECK OUT	NO. NIGHTS	TOTAL COST
Accommodation in Country X					
Town A	Accomm 1	19-Aug	21-Aug	2	00.00
o/night on train		21-Aug	22-Aug	1	00.00
Town C	Accomm 2	22-Aug	28-Aug	6	00.00
Town E	Accomm 4	28-Aug	31-Aug	3	00.00
o/night on ferry		31-Aug	1-Sep	1	00.00
Town F	Accomm 5	1-Sep	8-Sep	7	00.00
Town G	Accomm 6	8-Sep	9-Sep	1	00.00
Accommodation in Country Y					
Town J	Accomm 8	9-Sep	15-Sep	6	00.00
Accommodation in Country Z					
Town K	Accomm 9	15-Sep	20-Sep	5	00.00
Town L	Accomm 10	20-Sep	22-Sep	2	00.00
Total cost of accommodation					**00.00**

CLUSIONS	NOTES	TELEPHONE (+XX)
tel room, breakfast	confirmed booking 6/7	1234 5678
bin	confirmed booking 6/7	1234 5678
&B, access to guest kitchen	confirmed booking 6/7–info from VIC for finding house	1234 5678
partment	confirmed 7/7. Ring owner on arrival. He will meet us in front of the apartment building.	22501250, mobile nos. 1234 5678, 9503 9750
otel room, breakfast	confirmed 7/7, given credit card details to hold booking	1234 5678
		CODE (+XX)
ouse, includes linen	deposit paid, balance due 1 Sept	1234 5678
		CODE (+XX)
4 bedroom house	deposit paid 24/7–directions given	1234 5678
B&B	deposit paid 25/7	1234 5678

As well as the cave house in Granada and windmill in Portugal, we have stayed in a traditional fisherman's cottage in Norway, ancient stone farmhouses in the Dordogne and Tuscany, 1930s apartments in Oslo and Vienna – all wonderful experiences in themselves.

TRAVEL TIP
Just before leaving home, complete your 'Accommodation Details' spreadsheet and email it to yourself. If during your travels you, for example, lock yourself out of your accommodation and you have no means of contact on you, you can go to an internet cafe and retrieve the details. You might like to include in the email other information of importance.

POWER UP

Sockets, plugs and voltages vary from country to country so if you are travelling with electrical items you'll need to take account of the differences. You will need adapters to put between your appliance plug and a wall socket; you can buy these at airports, travel agents or travel-goods shops. These adapters convert plugs, but they do not convert voltage: your appliance and the local power supply must be compatible.

In Australia we use 240 volts; it's 250 volts in the UK and 220 volts through most of Europe. You can use your Australian appliances in these countries.

Some countries use 110 volts (including the US, Canada, parts of Spain, and Japan), half that of our supply. To use appliances in these countries, look for appliances that have 110 voltage, or even better, have dual voltage – both 220 and 110 volts with a converter switch. Failing that, you might have to buy battery-operated shavers and toothbrushes.

GUESTS AND HOSTS

Accommodation providers are selling a product; you're buying an experience. When you book accommodation with small operators, you are most likely to receive a warm welcome, a clean property, and all the help and advice you need. Small businesses usually have a tremendous commitment because it's not only their livelihood, it's also their life. And because they can't afford expensive advertising campaigns, they are highly dependent on repeat business and word-of-mouth recommendations. In all my years in tourism, I have known very few small operators who are not passionate about both their own product and the region in which they live. It's this passion that you are, in part, purchasing when you stay with a small business, as well as their genuine local information.

Your stay is a two-way contract, with obligations and responsibilities on both sides. Certainly the operator has the responsibility of presenting you with a product that matches their advertising and your reservation. You are entitled to expect a professional approach, and clean accommodation in which everything works.

On the other hand, you are a guest at their property, so keep in mind how you would expect a guest to behave in your home. Remember you are in a foreign country with different customs and habits. Don't be judgemental of difference; celebrate it as one of the key reasons for travelling. You might even pick up some good ideas for home.

An accommodation provider can expect that you will care for the property and leave it clean and tidy. They can expect that during your stay you will respect the privacy and rights of other guests and of the hosts if they live on-site (by not being noisy, or nosey, drying your clothes discretely, cleaning the public barbecue after use and so on). This sounds pedantic and authoritarian, but hosts' rights are abused frequently enough for the issue to be worthy of mention.

Small tourism operators the world over are usually working on fine margins to keep their prices competitive, so if you buy three-star, it is unfair to expect a five-star product. Your expectations should be consistent with what you have paid, and what you've paid is only relevant when compared with the competition in that area. The facilities and services of an apartment for $1000 a week in Paris will be very different from those of a house for $1000 a week in rural France.

Some of our best travel experiences have involved getting to know our hosts. From them we've learned insights about a place that we'd never have found in a guidebook or brochure. Their warmth, welcome and generosity have added a glow to our stay. During a stay in Hamnoy on the Lofoten Islands, our host gave Fred (who is a traditional boat enthusiast) a parting gift of an old fishing-net weight. It's a beautifully formed flat, round stone with a small off-centre hole to take a rope. Its hefty weight played havoc with our luggage allowance, but we were deeply touched.

For such occasions, we normally take a few small gifts in our suitcase (something Australian), along with some postcards of home, to leave a thank-you note behind at the end of our stay. Saying thank you is rare these days, which gives it real value and makes it especially nice to do.

We do this because we recognise the time, effort and goodwill that goes into providing a good tourism experience. We know that no matter how hard you try, things can still go wrong, but that isn't the same as deliberately trying to upset someone's holiday enjoyment. For this reason, the websites that list individual travellers' experiences (for example, Trip Advisor) need to be viewed with some scepticism. The opinions are subjective, and when you read of poor service or quality, you're only getting one side of the story.

Because nearly all operators try to do the right thing, we need to be tolerant when things are not perfect. Rather than aggression, which will jeopardise the guest–host relationship (in which the loser is more likely to be the guest), a simple request to fix a problem will usually be met with ready acquiescence. Don't leave it till check-out time to inform your host that the iron didn't work, or there was no hot water. Tell them at the time and give them the opportunity to rectify the problem. Stay calm when things go wrong – getting worked up will only cause you stress.

If you're fair but undemanding, return the small kindnesses offered and respect your host, your relationship will be transformed from distant customer to welcomed guest and you will reap many benefits.

You can start to build a winning relationship long before you arrive at your accommodation. How you word your emails can signal to the operator whether you are going to be a guest worthy of extra time and effort, or not. If you're inquiring about accommodation in a country where English is not the first language, but you can only write in English, start your message with an apology that your email is not written in the host's language. As English speakers we can be lazy because so many people around the world understand our language, but that does not give us the right to force our language on others.

Make sure there is warmth in your words as you ask about facilities and location, public transport and other issues. Keep in mind that this is all towards a better holiday experience for you.

Learning some of the local language will certainly break the ice. If your first greeting in person is in your host's language (even if you're lost from then on), it's a good start. Continue to use your host's language whenever you can (*bonjour*, *per favore*, *danke*, *si*), even if you know they can speak English perfectly. It's a mark of respect.

When you return home, if you have any positive suggestions for your hosts, send them an email. Feedback is the lifeblood of small businesses that can't afford expensive research.

STAYING GREEN

All the sustainable practices you adopt at home to conserve water and power should go with you when you travel. (It is estimated that while travelling, tourists use up to four times the amount of water that they use at home.) The temptation is to think that because you've paid for everything at your accommodation, you are free to use it as you wish, and you're wasting money if you don't use it – extravagantly in some cases. But leaving lights on unnecessarily, or leaving the heater on while out, or even using up the complimentary shampoo (and thereby creating more plastic to be disposed of) is abusing the environment.

Try to limit your impact on the environment in which you are staying. This means keeping your rubbish to a minimum by not purchasing food and other items in bulky packaging, and recycling as much as you can. When you pack your picnic lunch, use a small plastic box that can be washed and reused, and a sturdy water bottle that can be refilled, rather than adding the waste of another empty water bottle to the world. If you're concerned about the quality of the water, boil it first, or use water purification tablets.

Consider how you spend your money, and to whom it is going. When you choose locally owned accommodation, you are ensuring that your money stays in the region, rather than perhaps being siphoned off by a multinational to shareholders in another country. The same applies to the places you eat, the guided tours you select and the souvenirs you purchase.

WEB SEARCH
See **www.responsibletravel.com**, a web-based travel agent representing properties that meet responsible tourism guidelines

TRAVEL TIP
Be a green guest by following these guidelines:
- choose eco-friendly accommodation, or accommodation with a green rating
- keep rubbish to a minimum
- recycle where possible
- select biodegradable products for dishwashing and clothes washing
- don't use resources unnecessarily (lights, water)
- ask that your bed linen not be changed unnecessarily
- reuse towels
- don't use airconditioning when you can open a window
- put on a jumper instead of turning on the heating
- when possible, hang clothes in the sun and breeze rather than using a clothes dryer
- don't squander the complimentary soaps and shampoos if you don't need them
- don't collect or keep brochures unnecessarily; of those you do pick up, leave them at the property for future guests to use
- be alert to keeping your footprint small and light

5

MONEY MATTERS

When preparing to travel, lay out all your clothes and all your money. Then take half the clothes and twice the money.

Susan Heller

- Budgeting for ease of mind
- What does your bank offer?
- Card management
- Keeping track of expenses
- Be money smart
- Taxes
- Holidays don't put an end to bills
- The etiquette of tipping

BUDGETING FOR EASE OF MIND

Having tasted the excitement of planning, it's time to get down to the dry reality of affording your dreams. It might be tedious, and not usually your strong point, but careful budgeting will give you ease of mind and ensure you don't return home to unwelcome hardship.

To start, research the major costs – the airfares, accommodation, car hire – and put these into a budget. Together, these might make up 50 to 75 per cent of your total costs, depending on how thrifty you are, so add another 50 per cent (to be on the safe side) to these major costs to see what the likely total cost could be. This is the first reality check – can you afford this holiday?

TRAVEL TIP
Don't confirm or pay for any bookings until you have done at least the first draft of your budget and are confident that you can afford your holiday. It's easy to get swept up in the excitement of planning, letting your travel heart rule your financial head.

If all's looking good, start to fill in all the other costs of your holiday, including the following:
- food and drink – eating in, dining out
- public transport, taxis and transfers
- entertainment and activities
- spending allowance

For an indication of how expensive a country is to eat, stay and travel in, check recent editions of guidebooks for the destinations you will be visiting, as some guidebooks give indicative daily living costs. Ask among friends, too, for their experiences of the relative costs within countries. Food is always a major expense, and can vary enormously from one place to another; it also depends on how you choose to feed yourself. (I once asked an English butcher for lamb backstraps. When he finished laughing he asked if I wanted a quote first. We ate chicken that night.)

All this is to say that you can't afford to underestimate your daily contingencies, and while you need to travel on a budget, you don't want to be so frugal as to spoil your special holiday.

Use the budget and itinerary planning spreadsheet (p 104) to build your budget. Keeping track by destination allows you to take into account different contingency costs, and perhaps different activities you'll undertake, depending on the country.

If your total figure is ballooning out, go back to the costs where you can make savings (for example, lower your accommodation expectations, plan to dine out less frequently), and rework.

Because I'm not much of a shopper at home, and we live in the country where the consumer pressures are lower, I often feel overwhelmed, indeed panicked by the constant calls on my pocket when travelling. Spending is unavoidable, and while you can control the non-essentials, there are many costs you can't escape, and you do want to bring home a couple of special mementos. So don't underestimate the intangibles in your budget.

Once you have that final figure and know it's affordable, then it's time for take-off.

TRAVEL TIP
When you make your transport and accommodation bookings, you will most likely be required to pay in advance, either the full amount or at least a deposit.

Some pre-payment issues to be alert to:
- check the currency being quoted – if it's not Australian dollars, convert it so you understand the cost to you, and for entering in your budget
- ask how you are to pay – cash on arrival is always a little risky (will they hold the booking for you?). If they do want cash on arrival, be sure you have sufficient local currency to pay
- paying by direct deposit into an account is safer than giving your credit card details by email, unless the site is secured
- check the cancellation terms
- carefully file all receipts, vouchers and tickets, to take with you

WHAT DOES YOUR BANK OFFER?

Banks are very attuned to the needs of travellers, offering a host of services from loans and insurance to foreign currencies and overseas assistance. Most of the banks have travel sections on their websites.

When you're making your plans, alert your bank manager that you will be travelling overseas and that your pattern of withdrawal from your credit or debit card accounts will be different from usual. Give the manager an itinerary to show what countries you will be in on what dates. When the international section within a bank sees unusual spending patterns, they suspect fraudulent use of a credit card. Before stopping the funds, they will usually contact your branch manager to ask if they know of any reason for the change, or why sums are being withdrawn at Austrian ATMs. It makes life much easier if the issue is resolved at this point.

ITINERARY AND BUDGET

This spreadsheet helps to manage money and your itinerary (it ensures you account for everything). Visit The Five Mile Press website to download a form for your own use.

DATE	DAY	TRAVEL	DETAILS	OVERNIGHT
May	Fri 18	Depart Melbourne	QF123	in flight
	Sat 19	Arrive City A		
		Train to Town A	Eurail 8 days	
			Train 1	Town A
	Sun 20		*Accomm A*	Town A
	Mon 21	Overnight train	Train 2	on train
	Tue 22	Ferry to Town B (return ticket)	no booking required for	Town B
	Wed 23		*Accomm B*	Town B
	Thu 24			Town B
	Fri 25			Town B
	Sat 26	Ferry to Town C	Train 3	Town C
	Sun 27		*Accomm C*	Town C
	Mon 28	Train to Town D	Train 4	Town D
	Tue 29		*Accomm D*	Town D
	Wed 30			Town D
	Thu 31	Bus to ferry port	Bus	
		Overnight ferry	Ferry	on ferry
June	Fri 1	Arrive Town E	*Accomm E*	Town E
	Sat 2			Town E
	Sun 3		Train 5	Town E
	Mon 4			Town E
	Tue 5	Train to Town F	Train 6	Town F
			Local train return	
			Accomm F	
	Wed 6	Train to Town G	Train 7	Town G
	Thu 7		Train 8	Town G
	Fri 8		*Accomm G*	Town G
	Sat 9	Fly to City B	Express bus to airport	
			Low-cost carrier X	Town H
	Sun 10		*Accomm H*	Town H
	Mon 11			Town H
	Tue 12			Town H
	Wed 13			Town H
	Thu 14			Town H
	Fri 15	Drive to Town J		Town J
	Sat 16	Car hire 6 days	*Accomm J*	Town J
	Sun 17			Town J
	Mon 18			Town J
	Tue 19			Town J
	Wed 20	Drive to Town K	*Accomm K*	Town K
	Thu 21			Town K
	Fri 22	Train to City C		
		Train to airport		
		Depart City C		flight
	Sat 23	Arrive Melbourne		
		Miscellaneous transport		
		TOTALS		

MONEY MATTERS 105

RANSPORT	ACCOMM	FOOD etc.	PAID	VOUCHER	NOTES	TOTAL
XX.XX			yes	e-ticket	D 15:30	
					A 11:05	
XX.XX			yes	tickets	D 14:05, A 19:30	
	XX.XX					
					D 19:35	
XX.XX					A 09:10	
	XX.XX					
					D 12:20, A 22:10	
	XX.XX					
					D 16:10, A 20:13	
	XX.XX			booking form		
XX.XX						
XX.XX			yes	e-ticket	D 00:45	
	XX.XX				A 14:30	
					D 08:40, A 10:49	
XX.XX						
	XX.XX					
					D 12:25, A 17:32	
	XX.XX					
XX.XX					D 06:00, A 07:45	
YY.YY			yes	e-ticket	D 09:25, A 10:05	
	XX.XX					
XX.XX						
	XX.XX		$XX dep.	receipt		
	XX.XX		$XX dep.	receipt		
XX.XX					D 06:45, A 08:56	
XX.XX					D 09:10 A 08:56	
					D 12:20	
					A 19:55	
XX.XX						
XXX.XX	XXX.XX	XXX.XX				XXXX.XX

> **WEB SEARCH**
> Banks' websites outline their full range of services for travelling customers

Foreign currency

Your bank can supply you with foreign currencies, although rarely immediately across the counter. With the Commonwealth Bank you can order foreign currency on their website and collect it at your nominated branch. Other banks can take about a week to order it in for you.

If you don't order currency in advance, you can get it from the foreign exchange bureau at the airport. It is a good idea to have a small amount of cash for the country of your destination, to pay for taxis, coffee and other small items on arrival. Or simply withdraw local currency from an ATM in the arrivals hall of an airport. (It's a good idea to check first – we found that the ATMs at Marco Polo [Venice] airport did not recognise our Visa Plus cards – always cause for a racing pulse.) Taking a small stash of US dollars or UK pounds will give you a good fallback in most countries if you find you have no other access to funds.

Traveller's cheques

Again, these need to be ordered in advance, and you'll need to nominate the currency and the value denominations. If you're taking credit cards with you, it's probably best to have traveller's cheques in small denominations for small purchases or exchanges, and keep your credit card to handle the larger amounts.

You can use traveller's cheques like money, exchanging them for goods and services, or you can cash them at banks or foreign exchange bureaus. Be sure to check the exchange rates and fees – they can vary wildly. Hotels are likely to give you a much poorer exchange rate than you'd get at a bank. If you cash American Express traveller's cheques at American Express foreign exchange offices, there is no exchange fee. (Their website gives locations of their offices in each country.)

The benefit of traveller's cheques is that if they are lost or stolen, American Express (usually the provider) will replace them free of charge, normally within twenty-four hours. You must keep the receipt separate from the cheques, as the receipt will be needed for any claim.

When you cash traveller's cheques – at banks, hotels, some shops and so on – you may be asked to show some form of identification. This can be your passport, your driver's licence or your credit card. Beware of how you sign: some years ago in Rome, the manager in a bank where we tried to cash traveller's cheques refused to accept that the signature on Fred's driver's licence was the same as the one he had just put on the cheque.

TRAVEL TIP
It is legal to depart or enter Australia with any amount of money but you must report amounts greater than $10,000. You may also have to report traveller's cheques and personal cheques (known as BNIs – bearer negotiable instruments), irrespective of the amounts. For details, contact the Australian Transaction Reports and Analysis Centre.

WEB SEARCH
See the Australian Transaction Reports and Analysis Centre website:
www.austrac.gov.au > individuals > information for travellers

CARD MANAGEMENT

There is no doubt, credit and debit cards have made access to foreign currency very efficient. You can withdraw what you need, when you need it. All foreign exchange transactions attract a fee, but a bank's exchange rate is usually very competitive.

Credit cards
Cash withdrawals on credit cards attract interest from the transaction date until you have reduced your credit card balance to zero, so if you make only a partial payment on your statement, the bank will allocate that to purchases first, not cash advances. It is cheaper to use your credit card for purchases, and use a debit card for cash advances.

Most airlines and some hotels, restaurants and retailers will add a surcharge to your credit card payment, to cover their merchant fees (and in some cases, to add to their profit).

CHECKLIST
When planning to use your credit card overseas:

- ❏ notify your credit card provider that you are travelling overseas
- ❏ check with your bank that your daily and weekly withdrawal limit is sufficient; increase it if necessary
- ❏ check that your credit cards won't expire during your travels
- ❏ note the due date of your credit card payment
- ❏ consider having two credit cards, and keep them separate
- ❏ if travelling with a partner who has a card linked to the same account as your card, consider applying for a card with a separate account (a back-up if one account fails or your daily limit has been reached)
- ❏ ensure your credit cards are linked to accounts (credit, savings, cheque) in the way you want them to be
- ❏ check with your bank that your cards are suitable for use in ATMs in foreign countries – those that are usually bear the 'Plus' or 'Cirrus' logo
- ❏ from your bank's website, research the emergency contact numbers you will need in the event of your card being lost or stolen
- ❏ photocopy your credit cards and keep separately
- ❏ four-digit numeric PINs are a standard requirement at ATMs in most countries, so if your PIN includes letters of the alphabet, change it to all numbers before you leave home

WEB SEARCH
For the location of ATMs at airports, check the terminal maps of airport websites.
Both **www.mastercard.com/atmlocator**
and http://visa.via.infonow.net/locator/global
allow you to search any city in the world, and will give you a map of ATM locations

Debit cards

Not all debit cards work overseas in their intended fashion. If your credit card is linked to your savings and cheque accounts, and you select one of these for a merchant or ATM transaction, it may still treat the payment or withdrawal as a cash advance. Check with your bank.

Travel Money Cards

Some banks are now offering a form of debit or pre-paid card for travelling in which you can pre-purchase a range of foreign currencies, limited, however, to the most obvious – the euro, UK pound sterling and US dollar.

You buy currencies in advance, giving you the chance to avoid fluctuations and know exactly what value to budget for. The funds sit in the account for you to withdraw as needed, and can be topped up during your travels through funds transfer on the internet. The card is protected by a PIN number and is used at ATMs in the normal way.

It's another good travel tool worth asking about at your bank.

TRAVEL TIP
It's safer to use an ATM when the bank is open, so that if the machine does not return your card, you can go into the bank to retrieve it. In some cases, the bank won't have access to the card until the ATM is restocked; however, they will then retrieve it and if necessary forward it on to you.

KEEPING TRACK OF EXPENSES

Having developed a careful budget for your holiday, take the document with you to ensure you are living within your means. A budget is a good way to restrain you from shopping till you drop. Every possible purchase can be preceded with the question: 'Is this what I really want? If I buy this now and find something better later … ', or 'I know I can buy a shirt at home, but I'm unlikely to ever have the chance again of going to the opera at Teatro alla Scala.' Unless you have unlimited funds, there will always have to be choice, and your budget will be your guide.

TRAVEL TIP
- have a small wallet with pages to record your spending, and in which to keep all your receipts
- file receipts by currency
- keep all currency exchange receipts
- always request a receipt from an ATM when withdrawing cash (this will also give you your account balance, which is a good check on finances)
- regularly check your credit card statement online
- also online, you can check the exchange rate the bank is using for cash advances
- record the day your credit card payment is due and either arrange pre-payment before you leave home, or pay online on the due date (this needs to be set up; it is not standard)

BE MONEY SMART

Foreign currencies can be tricky to get used to. Some have so many zeros that you can feel fantastically rich – until you start spending. It's important to get used to the currency you're using – the look and feel of the different coins and notes. You can so easily make a mistake when paying for something, and not everyone is so honest as to correct your error. (Although surprisingly, many retailers are disarmingly helpful, sifting through the coins in your outstretched hand to extract the right amount.)

Before leaving home, print out the currency conversion rates you'll need and make up a small card that you can keep in your wallet for easy referral. Become familiar with making mental conversions to check prices, or carry a small calculator.

Language problems can be most apparent when being told what you owe for your purchases, especially at food markets. To overcome this, carry a small pad, calculator and pencil and ask the seller to write down the numbers. (This pad will come in very handy as you can also jot down key words from your phrase book to ask questions, or draw a picture of what you need to know about.)

TRAVEL TIP
When moving on to another country with a different currency, you can spend your remaining cash on duty-free items before departure. A much better option is to leave it with those airports and airlines that collect leftover currencies on behalf of charities, usually for desperately poor countries.

TAXES

Tax refunds

In many foreign countries, when you shop within pre-determined criteria, you can usually reclaim the sales tax (or value added tax – VAT) you've paid on goods. The requirement is normally a minimum amount spent at one outlet. It sounds terrific in theory, but some countries make it so difficult to reclaim the tax that you give up trying. And you must remember to ask for the documentation at the time of purchase. On the other hand, the savings can be considerable. The tax rate in Scandinavian countries is around 25 per cent; in the UK it's 17.5 per cent.

Look for shops displaying a 'Tax-Free Shopping' sticker on their window. When you make your purchase you'll need to show your passport, and the store will give you the paperwork for claiming. Most stores use the services of Global Refunds to process the paperwork; Premier Tax Free is the other company – the choice is the retailer's. You make your claim at the place of departure from a country. In the case of Europe, you make the claim at your final exit from all European Union countries.

At the airport:

1. have your tax-free documentation stamped by customs
2. have easy access to the goods for which you are claiming the refund (If the goods are not in your hand luggage, make the claim before checking in your bags)
3. hand over the receipts, the stamped tax refund documents and your passport at the refund services desk (they will probably want to see the goods)
4. get an immediate refund, or drop the documents into a special box at the airport (if you get an immediate refund, it will be in the local currency, for which you may have no need)

When you look at an airport layout map, locate the tax refund office. This might be a small cubbyhole tucked away in a deserted part of the airport, or it might be a service provided by the cafe in the departure lounge.

If you're not taking an immediate refund, it will appear as a credit in your own currency on your credit card statement some time in the future.

While it is supposed to be possible to mail the forms from home, in my experience the officials in the country where you're seeking the tax refund always have an excuse for not refunding. Somehow, there's always one vital piece of information missing …

Just a thought: if you've had cause to use a public service while in a country, for example, police or a hospital, you might choose not to claim the tax refund.

> **WEB SEARCH**
> For more information about tax refunds:
> www.europeforvisitors.com (general information)
> www.globalrefund.com
> www.premiertaxfree.com
> And for locating the tax refund office, have a look at the terminal maps on airport websites

Departure taxes

Australia is one of the few countries in the world that does not charge a departure tax. Of those that do charge a tax for leaving, it is often part of the price you have paid for your airline ticket. Some countries levy the airlines so that the tax cost is passed on to passengers within the ticket price. But some countries levy the tax on departing travellers, and nearly always in the local currency. In such cases, you need to be sure that you have sufficient local money to pay the tax. The concierge at a major hotel might be the best source of information about the need to pay departure tax.

HOLIDAYS DON'T PUT AN END TO BILLS

As part of your holiday preparations, you'll need to consider bills that will fall due while you are away. The easiest way to manage these is to register for internet banking with your bank well in advance of your departure date. In this way, you can pre-arrange for payments to be made on due dates, or pay while you are travelling. You can also transfer funds, and check your account balances and transaction history.

Most utilities allow you to set up direct debits so that you don't have to think about these bills while you're travelling.

THE ETIQUETTE OF TIPPING

For Australians, the act of tipping is not common beyond restaurant service and taxis, and can be an uncomfortable act, tainted as it is with the social stigma of casting largesse to the peasants. It can also be confusing and embarrassing if you don't know what and when to tip; and even how to hand over the money. On the other hand, social equity issues probably don't inhibit those on the receiving end.

In a time when we all search for bargains and special offers, tipping is an anomaly: that we choose to pay more than what is asked. And it normally comes at the end of the service, so as an incentive it doesn't make sense either. There is the question of whether a tip is a right or a privilege that has to be earned, yet it's common practice, and in some places, mandatory.

In many European countries, a tip of around 15 per cent is already built into the bill you receive. On top of this, if you want to reward good service, here are the usual guidelines:
- 15 per cent of the total bill for outstanding service
- 10 per cent for good service
- nothing if the food and service are not up to scratch

If the service and food are poor, it's worth mentioning the problem to the manager. This shows that you're not just being stingy, and provides an opportunity for the manager to right the problem.

TRAVEL TIP

If you don't want to leave a tip, draw a line through the 'Tip' entry on the credit card slip so that it can't be filled in later.

There is a website that gives you a guide to expected tipping in different countries: The Original Tipping page. If you're still worried about doing the right thing, there are also numerous books on the market that outline techniques on how to tip.

WEB SEARCH
For tipping guidelines:
www.tipping.org

6

WHAT AND HOW TO PACK

*He who would travel happily
must travel light.*

Antoine de St Exupéry

- Planning your wardrobe
- Your suitcase
- Your hand luggage
- Clothes for the flight
- While you're on the move
- Bearing gifts

PLANNING YOUR WARDROBE

Like all other aspects of successful travel, careful planning is needed for your travel wardrobe. Living out of a suitcase for weeks on end can be a bore, but with careful consideration of everything that goes into your suitcase, you can turn it into an art form. Because suitcase weight is of paramount concern, every item you pack needs to count, with nothing superfluous.

Start planning your wardrobe early. Write a list of the items that you want to take – what you already have and what you'll need to purchase. The best items to take away with you are those you already own and know are comfortable and suitable. Buy the things you need to purchase early, and wear them a few times to prove to yourself that they fit well and will last the distance of your travels (ie that the colour doesn't run in the wash, that the shoes don't cause blisters). I speak from experience: I was let down by a pair of black pants when the elastic gave way before I even reached Singapore. With that went the advantage of a spare hand.

Check the websites of the countries you'll be visiting to find out about the weather for your time of travel, and choose clothes to suit the temperatures and climatic conditions. Also be sensitive to the cultures of the countries you are visiting. If you're travelling to Muslim countries, wear loose, light cotton clothes with long sleeves and long pants. Apart from this being quite cool to wear, women will find they are more respected and treated better by the locals. Cleavage can be divisive.

TRAVEL TIP
Select clothes for the following:
- comfort
- versatility
- light weight
- colour coordination
- minimum washing
- crease resistance
- drip dry or quick dry fabric
- warmth or coolness as required
- the right number and size of pockets
- cultural sensitivity

And don't pack anything you haven't trialled.

You'll be wearing the same clothes over and over, from a very limited range, so make sure everything coordinates. Choose basic, simple items that go with everything else in your case. And stick to just one or two colour themes – the darker the better. Light colours need more washing; dark colours hide a multitude of sins. Black/taupe or navy/grey are good combinations. Reversible items are good for variety and double the wear before washing.

Choose clothes for comfort first, not fashion. Comfortable waists (elastic is great), natural fibres, fabrics with 'give', plenty of pockets – these are the features to look for as you plan your wardrobe. When your clothes are comfortable you don't have to give them a thought during your travels.

Let's face it, food is an important part of a holiday, and the sad fact is that it's almost impossible not to put on weight.

So all the more reason to avoid anything that's tight at the *start* of your holiday.

Choose, too, for versatility – clothes that are suitable for both casual and smart occasions; simple clothes that can be dressed up with the addition of a shawl or jewellery for women, a vest or jacket for men. Dark-coloured trousers can serve a range of purposes (better than light-coloured denim): team with a T-shirt during the day, and with a smart shirt at night.

Jeans have some serious drawbacks: if you have to wash them, they take an age to dry; it's hard to get into the pockets when sitting on the plane; and a wallet in the back pocket is a beacon to thieves. Pants with deep side pockets are good – check before travelling that things don't fall out when you sit down. Pockets in shirts are easier to use when sitting. Travel pants that have zip-off lower legs (to transform a pair of long pants into shorts) are hugely popular with European tourists. The pants usually have the added advantage of lots of safe pockets.

TRAVEL TIP
Take some old clothes that you won't mind ditching if you need room in your suitcase for the return journey.

Layering is the other key to versatility. Start with a singlet or T-shirt for hot weather or extra warmth, followed by a long-sleeve T-shirt (thermal for a cold climate), followed by a cotton shirt, followed by a vest, followed by a warm zip-fronted jacket (polar fleece is light and quick drying), followed by a wind- and waterproof jacket.

This approach is also a great help if you're travelling through multiple climate zones, for example, through Singapore or Hong Kong on your way to Europe. You can wear the 'under' items in the hot climate, and pile on the others for colder weather, rather than packing two separate wardrobes.

For warmth, thermal fabrics are ideal. Check out the range at adventure sport stores, as they stock for backpackers, where weight is even more important. Choose thermal items by their weight, warmth, flexibility for layering, and quick-drying qualities. Thermal leggings add considerable warmth for cold climates (as do warm hats and gloves), and thermal long-sleeve tops can be smart enough to wear as a top layer.

Take care in selecting your waterproof jacket. Be sure to wear it in heavy rain and strong wind before you travel, so that you know it is fully waterproof and wind proof. A hood is a must – more practical than an umbrella, which is a nuisance and takes up a free hand.

Natural fabrics are best for warm climates, and seersucker is ideal because it doesn't need ironing. Linen creases too easily, but some linen blends are drip-dry. Soft jerseys look great and don't crush.

Loose-fitting pyjamas can double as your workout outfit (providing your workout is not in public!). You really only need two pairs of shoes (one pair is even better if you're game) – a pair for walking and something a bit smarter. Wear the heaviest pair for the flight.

WEB SEARCH
- Google 'travel clothing' for companies that specialise in clothes suitable for travel, plus luggage and other accessories
- also search adventure sport stores' websites (they often have end-of-season specials that are perfect for the season you are flying to)

TRAVEL TIP
Buy your shoes early and wear them in. They are the most important item to get right: uncomfortable shoes will spoil your holiday because you will walk a lot. Buy from a specialist who will measure your feet and show you a range that meets your specific purpose. Select shoes that are (in order):
- comfortable
- suitable for your purpose and the climate
- waterproof (or capable of being waterproofed)
- lightweight
- smart (for example, dark-coloured walkers will be more versatile than white)

YOUR SUITCASE

There's a trick to travelling light and, once mastered, it will add ease and freedom to your holiday. A large suitcase is cumbersome, and a heavy suitcase is, literally, a drag. You can be sure that at some time during your travels you will be faced with a steep flight of stairs, a long walk or a need to lift your case up onto a luggage shelf (such as in a train). Choose a suitcase of a size that will enforce discipline on you not to pack too much, and only pack what you know you can carry. Coming out of the London tube at Sloane Square, there is a steep flight of steps up to street level. Halfway up the stairs, an elderly man was in tears as he struggled with the weight of his case. Commuters pushed passed him without a thought of stopping to help. I know it shouldn't be done, but Fred lifted his case to the top of the stairs, but then couldn't get it through the turnstile. There would be other stairs ahead in his travels.

Buy a good-quality suitcase; a cheap case is not worth the money and when it starts to fall to bits during your travels it will be a real nuisance. Choose a suitcase with good-size wheels and a handle. This makes walking a breeze. If it's your only item of luggage, except for a small backpack, you'll always have a spare hand, and a spare hand is very handy throughout your travels.

TRAVEL TIP
Choose a suitcase that:
- measures around 650 x 450 mm
- is robust (has a frame)
- has internal compartments
- has external pockets
- expands
- has provision for secure locking
- has good-quality wheels
- has a handle that extends to a length that is comfortable for your height
- is as lightweight as possible

Aim to pack to a maximum weight of about sixteen kilograms, so that you're well within the usual weight limit applied by airlines, with a good margin for shopping. This might require some practice, so don't leave packing to the last minute. Lay out all that you think you want to take, pack it and weigh your case – you're sure to be overweight first time around. So reconsider what you *really* need, and what can be jettisoned. This is where choosing lightweight clothing and coordinated colours makes a difference.

There are lots of things that you need to pack besides clothing, and you need to be just as ruthless in determining needs and selecting by weight and size. For example, give careful consideration to the items in your toilet bag. The best way to save space and weight is to decant creams and liquids into small travel containers, and keep the range to the basics. Remember you can always replace what you use up while you're travelling.

WEB SEARCH
www.gogogear.com.au has a wide range of travel-related products

TRAVEL TIP
Be sure to check the weight allowance on all flights you'll be taking. While the major carriers usually allow twenty kilograms, some smaller budget carriers are less generous (twelve to fifteen kilograms), and some cheap flights don't allow anything but carry-on luggage (flights designed for business travellers returning the same day). If you're over the allowance, it can cost a fortune.

There are a variety of different packing techniques; all have merits:
- lay clothes flat with as few folds as possible
- roll clothes tightly and secure with elastic bands (keeps your case very neat)
- roll similar items of clothes together (saves a lot of space)
- wrap or roll clothes in tissue paper to help prevent creasing
- pack clothes in zip-lock plastic bags, then sit on the bag to expel all the air (good for bulky items such as jumpers)
- purchase the plastic bags that expel air and vacuum seal

- wrap shoes in disposable plastic shower caps
- don't ever pack an empty container – it can be filled with something else, for example, stuff shoes with socks and underwear
- leave small items till last – those things such as scarves and underwear that can be stuffed into empty spots
- check and double check that all bottles containing liquid are tightly sealed, place bottles inside plastic zip-lock bags for extra protection against leakage
- use screw caps rather than pop tops that can open under pressure or altitude
- use the internal pockets of your suitcase to sort clothing and other items to save rummaging
- always pack in the same way, so you always know where to find things in your case
- consider what you might need when you first reach your destination – warmer or cooler clothes than you've worn for the flight, a waterproof jacket, gloves, hat – and pack these items on top, or in an outside pocket of your case, for easy retrieval before you leave the airport
- if you're staying somewhere for just one night, pack the next day's clothes on top so you don't have to rummage

TRAVEL TIP
If you're travelling with a companion, each pack one set of clothes in the other's suitcase, in case one suitcase is lost or delayed.

Be sure to label your suitcase, inside and outside, and lock it securely – combination locks are better than locks that require keys. Electric cable ties are a good way of ensuring your case is secure, and of alerting you to any tampering. If they've been broken before you collect your luggage from the carousel you'll know your case has been tampered with and you can alert the authorities.

Tie a bright tag or ribbon to your case so you can easily identify it on the luggage carousel (unless, of course, you choose a red ribbon like everyone else).

CHECKLISTS

These are must haves:

- ❏ passport
- ❏ tickets
- ❏ visas (if needed)
- ❏ insurance documents
- ❏ itinerary and budget printouts
- ❏ photocopies of the front page of your passport, credit cards and other documents
- ❏ guidebooks and maps (consider razor cutting out the pages that you'll need from your guidebook to save on weight)
- ❏ medications and prescriptions
- ❏ spectacles and spectacle prescription
- ❏ sunglasses

Some clothing items to keep in mind:

- ❏ sun hat (crushable) or warm hat
- ❏ gloves and scarf
- ❏ waterproof jacket with a hood
- ❏ shawl
- ❏ polar fleece jacket
- ❏ vest (multi-pocket vests are handy)

Other items that you might consider packing:

- ❏ books, crosswords, pack of cards
- ❏ diary/journal/notebook and pen
- ❏ small pad and pencil
- ❏ camera, memory cards and charger
- ❏ mobile phone and charger
- ❏ small torch
- ❏ slim calculator
- ❏ small hand compass

- travel-size binoculars
- small bialetti coffee pot (I find this indispensable)
- sharp knife and corkscrew (also indispensable)
- water bottle (the collapsible bladder type is lighter and easier to pack)
- plastic lunch box (doubles as a safe way to bring home fragile souvenirs)
- soap or soap leaves, hand wipes
- small sewing kit and safety pins
- some first-aid items (see p 138)
- sunscreen
- plastic zip-lock bags
- cloth bag for food shopping
- small bottle of laundry detergent
- compact travel hairdryer
- shaver
- chamois-style sports towel and/or facewasher (quick-drying)
- power-point adaptor (suitable for your destination countries)
- small kettle or element for boiling water (depending on your destination)
- pegless clothes line

TRAVEL TIP
Dental floss is not only good for your teeth. This amazingly strong thread can mend and tie in a variety of emergencies.

WEB SEARCH
The website www.packinglistonline.com lets you enter a range of variables (destination, time of year, purpose for travel etc) and then produces a recommended list of items to take. It's really more novelty than enlightenment.

If you're really careful – and adventurous – it is possible to travel with just one bag, suitable for carrying on board and weighing around six to seven kilograms. It takes great discipline to keep your luggage so light (and to avoid anything sharp), but it offers fantastic freedom when travelling. This is really only possible when travelling to a warm climate – winter clothes weigh so much more, and you need more of them.

A first-aid kit is important to include in your luggage. Depending on your destinations, your kit might include the following:
- basic medications for diarrhoea, constipation
- painkillers
- tube of soothing/antiseptic cream
- bandaids and bandages
- small feet sponge pads for relieving sore heels or toes
- small bottle of lavender oil for insect bites

If you're travelling to major cities, there'll always be a pharmacy close by, so you need fewer emergency first-aid items.

YOUR HAND LUGGAGE

There is a range of strict rules you need to follow regarding carry-on luggage. Check your airline's website for dimensions and weight limits, and what is and isn't permitted on board. Check this information close to your departure date, as world events can change security measures. Also check the rules of your transit and destination countries. For example, in some cases, no liquids (including moisturisers, toothpaste etc) are permitted, or are only permitted in limited quantity and packaged in a specific way.

You cannot take *any* sharp items in your carry-on luggage. This includes nail scissors, nail files, knitting needles and pocket knives. Make a last-minute check of your carry-on luggage before check-in for your flight so that, if necessary, you can transfer any offending item to your suitcase.

Keep your carry-on luggage as light as possible; when you're in transit you often have to walk for miles. (If you're already feeling a little fractious after the first eight- to ten-hour leg, a heavy bag won't improve your mood.) It simply doesn't make sense to carry on board anything you won't need during the flight or immediately on arrival.

WHAT AND HOW TO PACK 125

WEB SEARCH
- check the websites of *all* the airlines you'll fly with (long-haul carrier, code sharer, and any others) for their luggage allowance, what you can carry on board, and other relevant information
- at www.smartraveller.gov.au, go to 'Travel Bulletin' and follow the links to the countries that have specific rules about what can be carried on board

CHECKLIST

Include these items in your cabin luggage:

- ❏ fragile items
- ❏ valuables, including wallet, jewellery
- ❏ travel documents (passport, visas, tickets)
- ❏ pen (make sure it doesn't leak – put in a plastic bag if unsure)
- ❏ most recent currency conversion rates (produce a small chart) for the countries you're going to, including the transit country
- ❏ information you'll need at your destination (public transport details, address and phone number of accommodation, map)
- ❏ mobile phone
- ❏ medications and prescriptions
- ❏ spectacles
- ❏ book (and a crossword book with pencil and eraser is a good idea)
- ❏ water bottle (fill after you've gone through security if the airport restricts carrying liquids)
- ❏ basic toiletries as allowed (toothbrush, toothpaste, moisturiser, lip salve, hand lotion, deodorant in containers of 100ml or less)
- ❏ electronic equipment (but remember a laptop will be counted as one bag)
- ❏ an empty pillowcase (with this you can make a pillow out of anything – a spare blanket, a sweater or coat)
- ❏ you might consider a change of T-shirt, underwear and socks (not a bad precaution against lost or delayed luggage)
- ❏ be sure to label your bag – inside and out

TRAVEL TIP
- if you're using a backpack, choose one with multiple pockets, and pack your valuables in the pocket closest to your skin. When in a crowd or a queue, bring your backpack around to the front of your body
- use a money belt or neck pouch for your most important valuables (wallet, credit cards, passport)
- lightweight, gortex backpacks are good
- mini carabiners (climbing clamps) are useful for securing the zips of your backpack

A smart backpack of a size approved for carry-on luggage is a useful item. Use it as cabin luggage, as a handbag, as a shopping bag, for picnics and so on. For a day's sightseeing, pack it with the following:
- a bottle of water
- fresh fruit or fruit and nut mix
- sharp knife (for the cheese and bread you might buy for lunch)
- lip salve, sunscreen, hat
- guidebook, map and phrasebook
- binoculars and compass
- warm jacket and waterproof jacket
- crossword book, pencil and eraser to fill in the times when waiting for buses etc (we've tackled crosswords in the most amazing locations)

CLOTHES FOR THE FLIGHT

It's not a fashion parade, and if comfort is important throughout your holiday, it is doubly important during a long flight. Choose clothing that is loose, made of natural fibres, lightweight but with a warm top to pull on if necessary.

Wear your heavier shoes, but avoid tight shoes, especially boots. During the flight your feet and ankles will swell, and if you've removed your boots you might not get them back on.

Dress casually but decently. You are sharing space with strangers over a long period of time and it really isn't appropriate that you display large areas of bare skin. Singlets and very short shorts or skirts can be very off-putting to fellow passengers, so be fair to them. Be mindful that you may be sharing your flight with people from a range of cultures who might find scanty clothing offensive.

WHILE YOU'RE ON THE MOVE

Plan for a three-day cycle of clothing – what you're wearing, what needs washing, and what's been washed. Remember, you don't have to change your clothes every day. We're a bit particular about this in Australia, but it really isn't necessary.

If you've chosen fabrics that are quick drying, then laundering often is not a problem, and this means you don't need as many clothes. You'll find that adventure sports stores even carry a range of quick-drying jocks! Socks can take forever to dry, so choose a quick-dry range. Some thermal wear gear is made of fabric that doesn't absorb body odour, so it doesn't need washing so frequently.

It's a good idea to pack a small bottle of laundry detergent or soap bar for quick, small washes, and carry a large plastic bag in your suitcase so you can keep dirty or damp clothes separate from clean ones. It's worth folding even your dirty clothes to save space.

The benefit of staying at a destination for a few nights or longer is that you'll have the chance to wash your clothes. And the benefit of self-contained accommodation is that it often includes a washing machine.

TRAVEL TIP
- there are laundry sprays on the market that will freshen clothes and remove stains without the need for washing (see **www.gogogcar.com.au**)
- try to avoid fabrics that need ironing, and remember the trick of hanging laundered items in the bathroom to allow the steam from the shower to remove creases
- unpack whenever you can to air clothes
- leave your walking shoes on the windowsill of an open window overnight

BEARING GIFTS

The gifts you take to overseas family and friends can be far more innovative than a boomerang or tea towel. You'll want to make sure that the gifts are Australian-made, small and lightweight. Here are some gift ideas:

- have a look at the websites of the national galleries, as their shops are full of lovely Australian gift ideas, including books, bookmarks, card sets, jigsaw puzzles of famous Australian artworks, T-shirts, notebooks and coffee mugs
- the National Library of Australia has a shop with good gift ideas including very specific Australian books, and stationery
- consider packets of Australian plant seeds (check quarantine regulations)
- DVDs and CDs with an Australian flavour are easy to pack
- items such as key rings, soap or small toys are always popular
- Australian produce such as cheese, abalone, honey, tea, coffee, nuts and wine will be appreciated (check what you're allowed to take into a country). The Australian produce stores at main Australian airports have a good selection
- my favourite food gifts include boxes of pale pink Murray River salt, locally grown walnuts, and the beautifully boxed spices from Herbies
- visit craft markets and farmer's markets for other ideas

> **WEB SEARCH**
> For gifts:
> National Library of Australia (**www.nla.gov.au/onlineshop**);
> National Gallery of Victoria (**www.ngv.vic.gov.au**);
> Art Gallery NSW (**www.artgallery.nsw.gov.au/shop**);
> **www.herbies.com.au** for beautifully presented herbs and spices and other local produce

We once handmade a pile of pasta to cook for family in England. Seemed a good idea – lightweight and novel – but I had to live with semolina through everything in my suitcase for the whole holiday. Never again.

7

THE REAL THING

*The real voyage of discovery consists
not in seeking new landscapes
but in having new eyes.*

Marcel Proust

- Looking for meaning
- Seeing honestly
- Issues of authenticity
- The goose's golden egg
- Tourism's shrines
- Shoring up memories
- Being a welcome guest
- Ethical issues

LOOKING FOR MEANING

In his book *The Intelligent Tourist*, Donald Horne asks the question:

> *How, when we know so little about even our own culture, can we ever know much about people of different cultures – even when they are alive, let alone dead and fragmented into a mysterious past?*

He acknowledges that knowledge has always been fragmentary and speculative. But for the intelligent tourist he believes there's value in knowing a little bit about a lot when the alternative is knowing nothing about a lot.

There are two aspects to travel knowledge. One is to become familiar with the practical issues (how airports function, how to buy a train ticket in a foreign language, how to order the sort of coffee you want). To attach importance to these things sounds mundane, but such knowledge reduces much of the stress of travel, and frees us for unanticipated surprises. The other is to make travel thoughtful through curiosity and observation, to develop critical antennae so that we don't accept things at face value.

One can choose between 'horizontal' travel – lots of places, lots of shopping, lots of fast facts across a broad landscape – or 'vertical' travel, where we seek fewer destinations and sights, but more depth, interpretation and understanding.

It's against the backdrop of our times, of superficiality, consumerism, rapid communication and easy technology, that we seek some deeper meaning in the world around us. Yet depth, resonance and pausing to appreciate are almost obsolete virtues in the quick here and now. Effort is the thing we don't have time for. The reward of success is ease, rather than exploration. But to turn this on its head, even a little effort can transform our travels into a way of adding layers of knowledge that can lead to increasing meaning and purpose in our own lives.

It's the quest to see beyond the obvious, to understand, respect and appreciate, that makes travel so worthwhile. Thoughtfulness offers a counterpoint to the arbitrariness of mass tourism. What we see and experience doesn't have to be grand to be valuable. How it adds to our understanding and folds into our memory is what's important.

In Dubai, we turned our backs on the glitter and glitz of the gold market and rambled along the fragrant alleyways of the spice souk. We purchased plump vanilla beans, black peppercorns and ruby saffron, and knobbly rocks of frankincense and myrrh. On a cold winter afternoon in Metung (worlds away from the searing desert heat of Dubai) I can lift a chunk of coal from the fire and place it in a small pottery bowl with a shard of frankincense and be immediately transported to another world. I am reminded of the special characteristics of a different culture: the small arrow on the hotel room ceiling that points towards Mecca; the haunting cry of the muezzin calling the faithful to prayer.

SEEING HONESTLY

At its most basic, tourism is simply one culture looking at another. What tourists see is largely controlled and directed; the manufacturers of mass tourism in any country will pre-determine what is of value and what is to be hidden from view. As curious travellers, we need to keep an open mind when we approach famous attractions; to be constantly asking ourselves, 'Why is this so?' It's not sufficient to simply swallow the abridged histories in guidebooks or slavishly believe the propaganda of tourist guides. Try to see things in their context, which means seeing other, more mundane parts of the culture, too.

Sometimes, I've visited a famous place or looked at a scene and been dismayed that it has failed to touch me in any meaningful way. One may approach the iconic with an expectation of being deeply moved, only to discover a nagging feeling of 'So what?' Some attractions become famous in arbitrary and touristic ways and are not really significant at all to the people who live around them – so why should they be special for us? The important thing is to be prepared with as much knowledge as possible so that you can understand the history or purpose behind what you see. And then, accept your own honest reaction, rather than being intimidated by the overly confident claims of a guide who spruiks about the momentous importance of a place.

In Prague, a highlight listed in all the guidebooks is Wenceslas Square. Expecting something that might echo the kind-heartedness remembered from a Christmas carol, we found instead a long boulevard lined with shops: gathering winter fuel now has a whole new meaning. We remained unimpressed until we visited a museum that told the history of Czech communism. The museum (not in our guidebook) is small and unsophisticated by the standards of the major museums, but its lack of adornment in telling its bleak story lent greater authenticity. Wenceslas Square took on meaning once we'd seen footage of the Prague Spring uprising, when the military turned violently on civilians seeking basic human rights. We retraced our steps to the square, and stood below the balcony from which Havel announced the end of communist rule.

The growing problem with the icons of the world is that they are swamped by tourist hordes. Perhaps the way to solve this is for countries to identify more major attractions, to divide the numbers over a greater range of locations. But as things stand, you might just decide that seeing the *Mona Lisa* isn't worth the effort. You might choose to forego the tedious queuing and the loss of time that could be better spent combing back streets, finding beauty in the ordinary and everyday. Think of the miles and miles of corridors adorned with paintings and crowded with tourists that have to be borne to reach the Sistine Chapel, whereas Michelangelo's *Pieta* rests in a corner of St Peter's Basilica almost deserted by comparison, evoking more humanity than one can bear. And while some churches are magnificent most are ordinary and some downright ugly. Excessive Baroque trimmings, heavy columns, poor-quality paintings – one doesn't have to revere them, or even visit them, just because they're old.

The more you travel, the more you learn to seek out the lesser-known places, the stories not covered in the travel brochures. The world becomes a giant jigsaw puzzle; the jigsaw pieces are the places you visit and the knowledge you glean. The major sights are the easily identifiable pieces that you immediately put into place (the corner of a building, the fingers of a hand); the out-of-the-way discoveries have all the nuances and subtleties of the varying blues of the sky or reds of a gown. They are just as important to complete the picture – every piece has its purpose. Travelling becomes addictive as we keep seeking the next jigsaw piece to push into place in our understanding of the world.

ISSUES OF AUTHENTICITY

To glimpse the real, you need to have a grasp of what has gone on in the past: how this community, these buildings, this music, these cultural habits, this cuisine came to be. What waves of war and invasion, for example, have created multiple layers of different cultures that have melded into what you see today?

In Phil Cousineau's book, *The Art of Pilgrimage*, he recalls early travels to Egypt and his discovery of the pilgrim-poet Basho's words 'a glimpse of the under-glimmer'. The words reveal to him 'the deeply real that lurks everywhere beneath centuries of stereotypes and false images that prevent us from truly seeing other people, other places, other times.'

Determining what is authentic and what is invented is the quest of thoughtful travel. 'Is this real, or has it been created for tourists?' is a good question to ask yourself. But Brugge in Belgium is a good example of how complex the answer can be. Once a wealthy trading town, prosperity declined rapidly in the fifteenth century and, time-locked, history passed it by. Without the impact of industrialisation, Brugge's original town plan and architecture were preserved by default. It remained a forgotten backwater until 'discovered' by tourism after World War II, when it was spruced up and marketed as the Venice of the North.

It is a beautiful little town, partly because of the consistency of built form, unspoilt by succeeding waves of fashion. But for me, it's too sanitised to be a true reflection of its past. Tourism has brought trappings of prosperity that are inconsistent with its own story. The overwhelming number of shops selling lace reveals the blatant commercialism behind the display of history. But while the dinginess, grimness and stench of its earlier poverty would be more authentic, who would go to see such a place? Who would want to live there?

In an age of movement, of permeable borders between countries and mixing and borrowing of cultures, it becomes ever harder to find unique identity. Before easy transport, individuality was the result of isolation. Now individuality is usually only found in the remnants of the past, in the solid forms that last rather than the fluid intangibles of everyday living. So a building, a cobbled alleyway, a sculpture or painting may be our only means back to a time when a country's original characteristics were forged.

But the concept of 'original' is also ambiguous. After the Nazis destroyed Warsaw, the city was rebuilt to replicate what it had looked like before the bombings. Choices were made about what parts of architectural history should be copied. Paris's magnificent boulevards, which we think of as timelessly and archetypically Parisian, were in fact constructed by Baron

Haussmann in the mid-nineteenth century. His plan required the destruction of the medieval city and the displacement of 350,000 people, mostly the working class who had lived in the old quarters. His development destroyed, both culturally and physically, what had previously been the real city.

Pockets of preserved lifestyle can still be found. In Madrid we sat at the café in the Plaza de Oriente and as the evening descended more and more citizens filled the plaza and the streets around us. Young families strolled by, elderly women walked arm in arm, teenagers dashed by on skateboards. This is the ongoing practice of city-dwelling people still committed to their siestas and dining patterns, still living very publicly and late into the night.

In Brittany, some women still wear the region's tall white lace hats not as a costume to please tourists, but unself-consciously as an age-old custom. But as someone said, national costume is usually 'what the peasants were wearing when they were discovered by tourism'. Snap-freezing a particular period of dress is not necessarily representative of the fluid nature of any culture. We can be amused by the nonsense of men dressed as gladiators at the entrance to the Coliseum, or smile at the costumed Mozart look-alikes in Vienna, but what should we make of Scotland's tartans? Are we to accept the Victorian invention of tartan as the traditional dress of the Scots and hunt for our own clan's colours (even when we can't claim a drop of Scottish blood)?

One of the problems with tourism is that it is, by nature, upbeat, interested mostly in happy stories, or stories of vanquish and honour, not the dark histories of poverty and oppression. As travellers trying to understand the past, we need to balance the staged presentations with the lives of common people. A painting, monument or building usually only tells one side of a complex social history. In trying to delve for a more all-encompassing view of the past, we need to ask, 'Who is telling this story?', 'Who has been left out of this slice of history?' All stories, all histories, have more than one point of view. Those in power control the narrative, ignoring all the parts of a history outside their ideology, or disguising those parts too uncomfortable to be told. But the past is made up of a vast cast of players.

What about the working class, the women, the children, those of different ethnicity or different political or religious beliefs?

On the Isle of Skye, you can visit Dunvegan Castle, occupied by the thirtieth Chief of the MacLeod Clan. The castle is full of fine furniture and other displays of wealth, and there's a video that you can watch that all but denies the role of the aristocracy in the Highland Clearances. For contrast, visit the crofter's cottages at the Museum of Island Life at Kilmuir. There you'll find a realistic portrayal of the life of the poor, and on the day we visited, the icy-cold rain, low grey skies and gale-force winds offered a sharp insight into the tragedy that befell the peasantry. It was terrible to picture barefoot children walking through snow.

There are now many fine examples around the world of people who are honestly trying to understand and record the past – its dark side as well as its triumphs. You may find such genuine attempts in social museums, or you may find them at events that have been created for the locals, where tourism is not a prime consideration; events that are for residents to express their sense of self, their values and their beliefs.

At Roskilde, near Copenhagen, we went sailing on a Viking boat. Fred was green with envy when I was offered the helm and we flew out across the choppy Roskilde Fjord, pushed by a brisk breeze. The boat, like others at Roskilde, was a faithful replica of a traditional Nordic craft, and in the shipbuilding yard attached to the museum, boats are constructed using traditional tools and techniques. It's an honest attempt to understand one aspect of that nation's history, to uncover another detail that reveals something about themselves, not necessarily for tourist consumption.

The Lofotr Viking Museum at Borg on the Lofeten Islands is a replica of a Viking chieftain's longhouse constructed next to the remains of the original. The longhouse is furnished as it would have been over 1000 years ago, and experimental archaeologists work at recreating the clothing and tools of that time. We talked to one archaeologist who was stitching reindeer hide that she had treated with beeswax and cod liver oil to create a waterproof balaclava. This, she explained, would be worn by the man who skippers the Viking longboat on the nearby fjord.

But it was also an experiment, an attempt to understand ancient, lost skills. She showed us a replica of a chieftain's sword with a beautiful pattern on the blade made by forging many layers of different iron alloys. But she was not satisfied: she felt that they had not yet mastered the perfection achieved by their ancestors.

Mass-tourism attractions lie at the opposite end of the spectrum of rendering the past. The Jorvik Viking Centre in York contrasts starkly with the Lofotr Museum. The York museum recreates a Viking village for entertainment rather than for examination. Such entertainment can still be fun, provided we recognise that *fun* rather than knowledge is the purpose.

TRAVEL TIP

Try these books to help you become a more curious traveller:

- John Armstrong, *The Secret Power of Beauty*, Penguin UK, 2005
- Alain de Botton, *The Art of Travel*, Penguin Books, London 2002
- Phil Cousineau, *The Art of Pilgrimage*, Conari Press, Berkely, California 1998
- Donald Horne, *The Intelligent Tourist*, Margaret Gee Publishing, NSW 1992

THE GOOSE'S GOLDEN EGG

In Aesop's fable, an old woman owned a goose that laid a golden egg every day. Unsatisfied, she decided to kill the goose to reap all of the gold at once. But the dead goose was like any other, and the old woman's greed led to her own poverty.

The practice of tourism carries echoes of this fable. Most governments see tourism's income as an integral part of their economy: it has the potential to lay golden eggs. But in their scramble to meet the perceived needs of tourists, they often overlook the rights of their residents and the fragility of their environment, and thereby threaten the very things tourists come to see – they threaten their golden egg–laying goose. Taken to its unmanaged extreme, the crowds, environmental degradation, identity erosion and understandable hostility of local people can lead to tourism's decline.

Despite quite overwhelming crowds at some destinations, governments are still reluctant to determine when the 'house full' sign should be raised. Greater Venice has a permanent population of under 300,000 and an annual visitation of around 20 million tourists. With such imbalance, there is the risk of reaching a tipping point at which a viable, identifiable community is lost, replaced by little more than a theme park.

Many visitors go to Venice only for the day, contributing little to the economy, treating the city as a vast, free, open-air museum. How do the locals feel as they are forced to forego their own public transport, unable to muscle their way onto overcrowded vaporetti? The rising waters in San Marco Square represent only one type of flood that is swamping Venice.

Some countries are rising to the challenge of finding a balance between the economic value of tourism and the negative impact of vast numbers. Attempts at preserving the past in ways that enlighten tourists through good interpretation rather than trivialisation can be seen in places such as the Roman Baths in Bath, or Hadrian's Wall at Homesteads Fort.

Many years ago, on a bitterly cold, blustery Christmas Day, we packed eggnog and sandwiches and went walking along the track that runs beside Hadrian's Wall across the north-east of England. In sleet, we crouched behind the wall to consume our Christmas lunch. The bleak environment and hostile weather made the history of the wall all too real.

Thousands and thousands of tourists, over decades, have walked along the top of the wall itself, grinding history into dust. Now, a combination of careful conservation and corralling visitors into key sites is helping to safeguard this remnant of Roman occupation in the British Isles for future generations to also visit.

In some countries, however, the dependence on tourism is not tempered by guardianship. Bureaucrats charged with developing tourism strive to create what they think tourists want rather than finding ways to interpret the nation's treasures. This often results in copying attractions that appear to be successful in other places, thereby creating a hollow uniformity. Or sites and stories are invented that have little to do with reality or history, while the true picture of a place, including social, conservation and ecological problems, is kept from sight. Governments and big business invest money in facilities for tourists that may have no value or purpose for the people who live there.

The dilemma of tourism was highlighted when the German tour operator TUI purchased the Tuscan village of Tenuta de Castelfalfi. The village includes a golf course and elegant but crumbling villas. To the residents, TUI's acquisition presents a chance for a brighter future. The tourism dollars from the planned 3000-plus German visitors a year will restore those crumbling villas and may bring employment for the locals. While tourists want to see the past preserved, residents want to live with all the benefits of the present. But it does beg the question: what is an Italian village if it is owned and operated by people of another nationality?

In rural France, partly as a response to cheap airfares from Britain, the British have gradually been purchasing and restoring more and more old, abandoned French farmhouses. Now, wandering around the delightful *bastide* towns in south-west France, the language you're most likely to hear is English, the faces decidedly British. Yet the French chose to leave those nostalgically charming farmhouses for more modern, efficient designs; it's the English tourists who have enabled the conservation of architectural identity. It's another cultural dilemma caused by tourism.

Of course, tourism isn't the only culprit in cultural and environmental damage. Globalisation, television and the internet, advertising and agricultural reform are just some of the other contributors. Perhaps it's just that mass tourism is a most visible symptom of change.

TOURISM'S SHRINES

Despite their overwhelming prominence in guidebooks, museums, cathedrals and palaces are not necessarily the most important cultural markers, just the focus of tourism. Some sights are so synonymous with a place that seeing them somehow equates with having 'done that city'. The Louvre, Versailles, Notre Dame – the country they're in doesn't even need to be mentioned.

Look beyond these celebrities and you'll find a world of wonder and beauty: the steel structure of a nineteenth-century railway station, the pleasing sweep of a streetscape, the rattle of stones on a chesel beach, or the abundance of different plants that make up a hedgerow. There are many threads in the fabric of a place – some broad swathes of bold colour, others single strands of luminosity.

Small discoveries can be as enlightening as celebrated works. A walk along the wealthy streets of the 16th Arrondissement in Paris will reveal to an alert eye beautiful Art Nouveau touches on door handles and wrought-iron gates. Such art sits alongside more dog grooming parlours than you're likely to see anywhere else in the world.

The streets are full of colour and history if you open your eyes. One morning in Gubbio (Umbria), waiting for a truffle fair to open, we walked up the hill towards St Giovanni church. Looking up to the immensely high church tower we spotted young men swinging freely on the bells, testing the tune and adjusting the clangers. For a brief time, their special skill (and lack of concern for occupational health and safety) brought the thirteenth century back to life.

Such sights are imbued with the touch of reality, there for their own sake, not for tourists. There's no museum shop to comb for souvenirs to confirm what you saw. You'll simply have to store the image away in your mind, for your own joy of recall.

Having said all this, those celebrity sights are still worth seeing – just try not to take them at face value; look for the wonder in them.

Museums and galleries are favourite sites for tourists, but these hallowed places can be intimidating to the uninitiated, hushed, as they are, with their own carefully defined cultural rules and protocols.

Most museums have a purpose that is culturally significant to their country: to guard important works of art (art galleries), to record how people lived in the past (social museums), to trumpet a nation's conquests (maritime museums), and so on. All are based on classifying a wealth of objects in a predetermined way that suggests order. For this reason, they present us with a digestible experience, without the clutter and jumble of life on the outside.

But they can be overwhelming – so much to be looked at, so much to absorb and try to understand. It simply is not possible to take in, for example, all the works at the Hermitage in St Petersburg, or all the exhibits in the British Museum. Or at least not if we want to view the works in a way that might foster some intimate response or understanding.

Museum visits can be just a shuffle past untold pictures, or they can be an opportunity to learn. The audio devices are good tools to help you notice detail and technique, but I find the information written on cards beside works of art or the large-print texts on the walls mystifyingly difficult to take in.

Art galleries are repositories of important works of art for their own sake, not necessarily related to the history of the country that holds them. We go to see them, acknowledging this lack of relationship, because they are unique. But artworks that belong to the heritage of a nation offer something beyond themselves; they can give us insights into the country's past – what was important, how people dressed, their battles and their religions. You might confine your museum visits to one or two artists who lived and worked in the country you are visiting, and tell that country's story. For example, Rembrandt's paintings in Amsterdam's Rijksmuseum are both magnificent and historically informative. Goya's war etchings in The Prado in Madrid record the harrowing story of Spain's fight for independence in the eighteenth century. You can study the raw emotion of his art, then go out onto the city streets and try to imagine how people survived such horror.

TRAVEL TIP
Use your museum visits to extend yourself, to learn:
- prepare yourself with research
- seek out the works of a nation's most important artists
- look for paintings or statues of world renown
- study the works by the same artist across a range of museums

- immerse yourself in the works from one period
- expose yourself to art you don't understand and try to find a way into its mysteries
- be prepared to commit yourself emotionally to what you're seeing
- think what the reaction might have been to a now-famous painting when it was first presented
- know that there is more to a precious work of art than what initially meets the eye
- don't let your opinion be influenced by the commercial value of a work of art
- look at famous works with a fresh eye, not with the eye that saw the work in a brochure
- acknowledge that there are no absolute rules for judging art, but that a commitment to observation and learning will lead you towards a deeper appreciation

History and art are not confined within the walls of imposing edifices. In Vienna, when the city walls were demolished in the late nineteenth century, Emperor Franz Joseph initiated the construction of the Ringstrasse – a wide boulevard that circles the old town. In place of the city walls, monumental buildings were erected to celebrate the empire, including the Parliament House, the State Opera, and the museums of fine art and natural history. By catching the Ringstrasse tram, you can travel around this beautiful boulevard taking in the triumphal splendour of the architecture: a solid historical record of the once-powerful Austro-Hungarian monarchy.

The Henry Moore sculptures dotted around the lawns at Louisiana near Copenhagen are phenomenal. Their dark, bulky shapes are thrown into relief against the wide green lawns and deep blueness of the Sound. The Danes picnic companionably in their shadows.

The Angel of the North stands on a hilltop at Gateshead in the UK. Artist Antony Gormley used his own body to model this twenty-metre-high angel. Its outspread aeroplane wings cant slightly forward in a beckoning embrace. Perhaps it's the convergence of 'humanness' and 'angelness' that lends such potency to the sculpture, but I find I can't drag my eyes away from its bold humanity and confident serenity. It always stirs me in some deep, essential way.

Public displays of the past come in all shapes and sizes. I have a favourite museum in Northumberland: the Lifeboat Museum at the mouth of the Tyne River. It exists to celebrate, very simply, the lives of ordinary people who did extraordinary service, and to preserve what matters deeply to them. The man who takes our money and tells us about the relics has lived through many rescues, and from an upstairs window, looking out across the North Sea, I can picture the acts of heroism of these simple fisherfolk.

Cathedrals

When visiting the famous cathedrals of the world, we may go armed with a respectful admiration, but are we seeing anything more than just another tourist sight? Are we touched by the religion, or moved to reverence by the grandeur of the architecture or the splendour of the art? The lack of the devotional robs a church of its purpose, but worse, we have watched young backpackers in Notre Dame flicking baptismal water at each other. Their behaviour was disrespectful; their poverty of connection or sense of place unholy.

Beyond the religious significance, as architectural wonders cathedrals remain unchallenged, their settings often awesome. It's worth trying to imagine the degree of cutting-edge architectural and engineering expertise these mammoth buildings represent. But for me, a more enticing picture to think of is what they must have looked like, soaring towards heaven, filled with precious objects and cherished relics, to the peasants in their hovels bowed down by the drudge of everyday survival. How their hearts must have lifted to the notes of a Gregorian chant, their eyes opened in wonder at the beauty of a stained-glass window.

I particularly love the crumbling remains of ancient abbeys wrapped in their blankets of silence, with tumbled walls pierced by blue skies, and bright grasses poking through disintegrating stonework. If you look carefully at nearby villages, the cottage walls are often patchworked with dressed stones carried off from the site.

Palaces and stately homes

Visiting the grand homes of the aristocracy gives a glimpse of a different way of life, opulence unknown to most people. It can be instructive about the past, but it's a very narrow view of a nation's history and one might ask who paid the price for such power and wealth. What was life like for others? What did it feel like to be a servant or a common soldier?

While some stately homes are vulgar, many are very beautiful. The perfection of Palladian-style architecture, the lushness of exotic furnishings, the collections of art, the fascination of the downstairs kitchen and scullery all make these places worthy of a visit for what they are in themselves. For contrast, you can usually enjoy your simple picnic lunch of bread and cheese in the extensive, manicured gardens.

The impression given by the Ringstrasse of pomp and splendour of the last Austrian Emperor Franz Joseph is complicated by a visit to the Schonbrunn Palace. On the guided tour we passed through rooms full of elegance, artwork and exquisite furniture. Then we came to the Emperor's private rooms. They were simple to the point of being almost bare in comparison with the rest of the palace. From an ordinary desk, the Emperor tackled his enormous workload, starting each day at 5 a.m. In one corner was a small bed, almost a camp bed, into which he must have fallen exhausted each night. On the wall was a photograph of his only son, who committed suicide at the age of thirty. These small nuggets of reality breathed more life into the Emperor as a real person than all the grandeur of the palace and the Ringstrasse.

There is something tragic about the way some of the grand statements of power and wealth have become no more than tourism sideshows. Consider how tourism's devouring superficiality has changed the Changing of the Guard at Buckingham Palace from an expression of Imperial power to crowd entertainment.

Castles are another matter altogether. Built for displays of force and protection, not comfort, they were usually vast, draughty and basic, and now, they are mostly in ruins. Along with your guidebook, when you visit ancient castles it's worth taking with you in your mind the opening scene of *Hamlet*, with its portrayal of intense cold and foreboding menace. At Warkworth

Castle – once home to Harry Hotspur of Shakespearean fame – we witnessed a display of clashing centuries. Warkworth was the site for the Battle of Shrewsbury in the fourteenth century. On the day we were there, low-flying fighter planes thundered overhead, the sound of modern warfare reverberating against the ancient castle walls.

SHORING UP MEMORIES

Tourism and photography have long been bedfellows; in fact, they have grown up together and become inseparable. The camera was developed in the mid-1800s, at the same time as railways introduced fast and reliable travel and Thomas Cook launched his first package tours.

Cameras are now the ubiquitous symbol of tourism and few travellers leave home without one. Even if you're not a great photographer, the pictures you take can be triggers for memories, and wonderful to share. But photographs can be limiting, too. They record the moment, the monument or the vista; their taking is essentially a passive act that is often a substitute for contemplation or an attempt to understand.

The problem with cameras is that they are often inadequate to capture a special moment. Walking along by the viaduct in Paris, we could hear the rich, full voice of a tenor, which we thought was being broadcast from the nearby Opera de la Bastille. The sound got closer and louder, and then a jogger dashed past, leaving behind him a string of stirring notes from Verdi's *Aida*. A camera could not have captured that.

There are many things a camera cannot record: the watery pink dusk settling over Venice, the low grey clouds blanketing the Highlands in Scotland, or the unrelenting greenness of Ireland. And not just sights. A camera can't capture a warm welcome, the spicy taste of Spanish tapas, the fragrance of incense in an old stone church, or the eeriness of the Roman catacombs. It can't capture the memory of a conversation, the goose-bump feeling when the air fills with the sound of carillon bells, or the moments of sheer happiness that wash over you just because you're lucky enough to be travelling.

> **WEB SEARCH**
> Along with your camera, think about keeping a journal.
> Instructions for making your own journal:
> www.fiveandahalf.net/blog/from-prints-into-journals

While we focus on *sight*seeing as the tourist preoccupation, sight is only one of the senses we need to engage. We should extend our travel vocabulary to account for tasting, hearing, smelling and touching. Being alert to the myriad sensual experiences of travel requires an active mind. Getting experiences to stay in our memory (rather than on a disk) takes practice: practice in the art of contemplation.

Learning to be observant is not easy. In our everyday lives of familiarity and rush we develop a mechanism of habitual seeing. When faced with something that is outside our everyday experience, we either fail to register the difference, or don't comprehend what we see. In the early years of touring, before the camera took hold, sketching was considered a normal way of recording what was seen. Like writing, sketching requires greater observation and interpretation than the casual eye used to take a photograph. Travelling with a journal, to record your experiences in words or sketches, will help to train your eye.

You see something sublime, then try to capture it in words: not just the physical appearance but the effect it has on you. Then you need to look again, and dig into your soul to try to articulate how you feel, try to explain your response to a sight. Ask yourself 'Why?'. It requires emotional honesty to go beyond the worn-out phrases of travel brochures, to find a meaning that is uniquely yours. It's an opportunity to question your own beliefs and prejudices, to hold them up for scrutiny as you record your personal discoveries. And you will reinforce your memories.

Photographs can be a barrier to thoughtful travel. All those well-known images in brochures and advertisements limit our ability to see afresh. Our eyes simply register a replica of the brochure's photo and our mind is denied a more critical, unencumbered and untutored appreciation. All the world's main 'sights' have been photographed ad nauseam; even a particular perspective becomes the norm. And then, by comparison, the real thing can seem so disappointing rather than being rare and unexpected.

You can hardly move on the bridge on the Riva degli Schiavoni as tourists jostle and crane their necks to take photographs of the Bridge of Sighs, a sight reproduced in nearly every brochure on Venice, from just that angle. On the far side of the Grand Canal you can uncover beauty and mystery in almost deserted narrow alleyways – places that never make it into the brochures.

We need to unlearn all the mass-produced, clichéd images, or block them out of our vision, so that we take an untainted eye to everything and come to an appreciation based upon our own honest responses rather than the direction of others. This requires a heightened level of attention, something greater than what we would normally practise at home. A camera will get in your way if you treat it as the master of sightseeing. Treat it, rather, as a tool of travel and make it just part of the experience. Practise taking photos that are at complete odds to the clichés; take joy in your artistic creations.

When we see beauty, we have a desire to possess it, to take it into our being, to add to our own expressions of the world. But it can't be possessed, and even capturing a scene in your camera won't make it yours. Instead, try to understand *why* something moves you. I've always found the clover-leaf motif in the stone windows of Venice particularly beautiful without being able to work out why. I have a copy of the motif on my desk, patterned onto a small cardboard box, but that doesn't help with understanding. Nor will a photograph ever reveal what lies behind an emotional response.

We never travel with a camera, yet my mind is full of images that I can recall at any time, without the need to riffle through a box of photos. And while we don't buy souvenirs as such, we have over the years returned home with simple mementos. In Cefalu, I needed clothes pegs – domestically mundane, I know, but the ones I purchased were big and carved, and even now, years later when using them to hang out the washing at home,

I catch a memory of a crescent-shaped harbour glimpsed through laundry strung across cobbled alleyways.

None of this is to say that you shouldn't take a camera. Indeed, photos are precious keepsakes. But so are the images you commit to memory, and they're much easier to draw upon at any time, in any place. If we acknowledge that 'being there' is far superior to seeing a photograph in a brochure, then your own photos alone might be too limited to truly help you recall your experiences.

TRAVEL TIP

- buy postcards of the main sights — professional photographers have the advantage of choosing the time to photograph, without the crowds, litter, traffic and grey skies
- treat your camera for what it is — only one of many contributors to shoring up memories
- take photos to recall difference: a small architectural motif, poppies glowing red in a field of wheat, the slant of sun on a dry-stone wall or glistening fish laid out in a fish market
- photograph the things you might want to reproduce at home: the design of a trellis or the patterning of paving stones, or how a dish was served in a restaurant
- rather than planning to buy your camera duty free, it's safer to buy before you leave, to check that it works properly

WEB SEARCH

for choosing a suitable camera:
www.dpreview.com or
http://photo.net/equipment/travel-camera
tips for taking great photos:
www.creativematch.co.uk/viewnews/?92664 (this is excellent, and you can buy the book); or
www.i-to-i.com/resources/general/perfect-photo.html

TRAVEL TIP

To record your experiences in words:
- buy postcards of sights that have moved you and on the back record your impressions and feelings, reactions and experiences relevant to the image
- be critical of what you see, rather than seduced by the celebrity of a sight
- write your travel stories with an audience in mind; it will force you to be thoughtful about language
- don't expect perfection, write about all aspects of your travels
- record anecdotes and small everyday acts
- include the stubs of bus tickets, museum passes etc in your journal
- in your journal sketch ideas that you want to take home

BEING A WELCOME GUEST

No matter where your travels take you, at one level the experience will always seem everyday and banal. In the cities you visit, people are simply going about their ordinary lives, and you see no more than you would at home. You register the lack of the exceptional and exciting, but to make it otherwise would be to rob the locals of their own reality. Foreign places are not (nor should they be) theme parks created for tourists any more than your own city is; they are living, breathing, working communities.

Similarly, the people who live in foreign countries are not actors in a sideshow, they're nothing more or less than fellow human beings. They might do things differently, usually for a good reason, and moral judgements ('that's not how we do it …') have no place in seeking to understand customs that are not our own. Coming to understand a different way of life, a different cultural ordering of the world, is at the very heart of the purpose for travel. Tourism has many downsides, but the opportunity to learn to respect cultural difference by seeing it work in its own setting is surely tourism's most valuable contribution. As Mark Twain said, 'Travel is fatal to prejudice, bigotry, and narrow-mindedness.'

Most of us travel with a sense of entitlement. We've worked hard, saved carefully and planned well for the chance to go and look at other people, their homes and their ways of life. But rather than entitlement, we should consider the opportunity a gift, and treat our host countries with our deepest respect.

Each month, more than 400,000 Australians travel overseas, and even though each one of us likes to think that we are the one genuine, thoughtful tourist, in fact many people travel with a high degree of goodwill and an alert interest and desire for knowledge. What we all need to be mindful of is that goodwill alone is insufficient if we are to lessen our impact on host communities. We need to also practise a high degree of responsibility.

Some dos and don'ts of responsible tourism

DO
- travel with some knowledge about the places you visit
- acknowledge that the rights of residents should come before those of tourists
- respect local beliefs, laws and values
- appreciate all cultures, even those that seem strange
- learn some basic words in the local language, especially 'thank you'
- respect people's privacy
- smile, say thank you, practise simple courtesies
- conform to the local dress standards
- follow (or exceed) environmental practices
- behave in a way that you would expect others to behave in your own neighbourhood
- behave in a way that helps ensure future travellers will be welcomed
- make generous donations at sites you visit that have a donation box instead of a gate ticket
- choose locally-owned tour operators, transport, accommodation, shops etc wherever possible
- turn off your mobile phone if taking a call will intrude on others

DON'T
- treat locals as if they were part of an act
- stand out as a tourist not responsible for what happens locally

- flaunt wealth
- lose your cool with people if things go wrong, as if local people belonged to an inferior race
- demand or expect similarities to home
- take photographs of people without their consent
- take photographs when you're expressly asked not to

ETHICAL ISSUES

In addition to responsible travel, there's also the issue of ethics. Do you want to travel to a country, deposit money with a regime, whose practices you do not approve of? Human rights abuses, corruption, condoned child prostitution, aggression – any number of political or social practices may cause you to consider not travelling to a destination, making your own private stand against what you believe to be wrong. You may not make a difference, but you may certainly feel that you've been true to your own values.

Some travel companies, such as Intrepid Travel, are good examples of ethical tourism practice, ensuring that tourist dollars reach local people, that cultures are not portrayed as sideshows, and that small communities don't become dependent on tourism income alone. In western developed countries, the impacts might not be as stark as they are in poorer nations, but that does not lessen the obligation to be ethical. Part of the act of thoughtful travel is, in your early research, to go beneath the veneer of what a country overtly shows to the world. If you don't like what you find, you can make a decision not to support those who perpetrate unethical practices.

8

ON THE MOVE

*Maps encourage boldness. They're like cryptic love letters.
They make anything seem possible.*

Mark Jenkins

- Travelling companions
- Finding your way around
- Keeping safe
- Keeping in touch
- Consular services
- Time out
- There's more to travel than shopping
- Shopping green

TRAVELLING COMPANIONS

Many years ago, Michael Gerber wrote a book titled *The E Myth*. He argued that it was a myth that most people who are good at something, for example plumbing, have the entrepreneurial skill to run a plumbing business. He also wrote that even the smallest businesses need the same divisions of labour and responsibility as big business: someone has to be assigned in charge of the accounts, in charge of production, in charge of marketing and so on. I think this approach can be extended into the art of companionable travel.

Many skills – from budgeting to map reading to using a camera – are needed for travelling. If you're travelling with a partner, work out who is best to do what job, assign each task and leave that person to call the shots (even if you have to sit on your hands and zip your lips). This will create a good working partnership; it will help avoid duplication and oversight, and it guards against one person being left with an unfair burden.

Travelling is not all beer and skittles. Jet lag, an unhelpful train conductor, a slightly grubby room, a missed connection – these and many more typical travel experiences can make you a less than pleasant companion. Keep in mind that the easier travel becomes, the more we fuss over small frustrations. Accept them for what they truly are: not life threatening, just tiny annoyances.

TRAVEL TIP
- don't set your expectations too high, so you're not constantly disappointed
- recognise that travel can come with problems, and accept them as part of the experience (they're the experiences most likely to morph into funny dinner-party stories)
- make time for yourself – a walk alone, time to read, to do some exercise or linger over a coffee

FINDING YOUR WAY AROUND

Guidebooks offer good information, and specific city guides even more so. Check out Luxe and Wallpaper guides; these somewhat hip guides are compact and necessarily brief on information, but they're good prompts for cities.

TRAVEL TIP
Keep in mind that your southern hemisphere instincts for direction will let you down when in the northern hemisphere. A small handheld compass is a real asset.

Tourist information centres offer a wealth of free advice and are your best first port of call whenever you arrive in a city. They are usually located in prominent positions close to central railway stations, and at some airports, and they are always shown on maps and guides. Tourist information centres offer:
- city maps
- accommodation advice and bookings

- transit maps
- public transport advice, and sometimes tickets
- city discount cards for public transport, museum entries etc
- tour advice (city tours, day tours) and bookings
- advice about things to do and see
- advice about current performances and events
- postcards and souvenirs

City tours – usually by bus or boat – are a good way to get a feel for a city. The commentary usually includes a potted history with corny jokes, but the overview will help to orientate you and to decide what you want to explore in more detail.

TRAVEL TIP
If you're over sixty years (or sixty-five in some countries) you can use your Australian Seniors Card for discounts at attractions, museums, theatres etc. Always ask.

Before heading out for your day's sightseeing, check your map or guide to get the lay of the land, so that you're not continually stopping to work out where you are, and thereby advertising that you are a tourist. You can also plan a route that flows easily from one sight to the next.

If you hire a car that doesn't have GPS, study a map before you enter an unfamiliar city, taking careful note of one-way streets and dead ends. Driving in heavy traffic, on the opposite side of the road, with signs in a language you don't understand, can be very stressful; so much more so if you're not prepared.

TRAVEL TIP
There are any number of high-tech mapping and guide options now available.
- use a portable GPS, or purchase a mobile phone that includes GPS
- download the relevant maps before leaving home
- when hiring a car, ask for it to include GPS
- if you have an iPod, you can download Sony's Passport walking tours for many cities
- for your portable MP3 player, you can download video guidebooks
- look for city guide podcasts

> **WEB SEARCH**
> For downloadable guides, see
> www.roughguides.com/podcasts and
> www.heartbeatguides.com

KEEPING SAFE

We are spoilt for safety in Australia, but in many parts of the world, gangs make their living from unwary tourists whom they consider to be legitimate targets for the redistribution of wealth. Bands of gypsies are highly organised, their practices choreographed as one group distracts while another robs. Keep your eyes peeled, especially in crowded places such as railway stations; don't allow people to bump into you and don't be distracted by groups of children making a scene.

Before you go
- check travel alerts for your destinations
- study your destination, its laws, customs and climate
- take appropriate clothes, both for the climate and the customs
- leave your travel itinerary and contact details with a family member or friend
- if you have a serious health condition or allergy, wear a Medic Alert bracelet or necklace

> **WEB SEARCH**
> See www.dfat.gov.au/geo for country-by-country guides to local laws, safety, health issues, and where to seek help

Prepare your mobile phone
It is now routine practice in many countries (including Australia) that at a time of accident or emergency an emergency services worker will look for ICE (In Case of Emergencies) numbers on the victim's mobile phone.

To record ICE telephone numbers in your mobile phone's address book, enter the word ICE and the telephone number of your next of kin. For more than one emergency number, use ICE ONE, ICE TWO, etc. You might record other details against ICE listings, such as your blood type or allergies. For this to work, your phone should not require a password for access.

Also in your mobile's address book, add the telephone numbers of relevant overseas consular offices.

Be familiar with the emergency number to call in the countries you'll be visiting (ie the equivalent to 000 in Australia). The number 112 applies in the United Kingdom and most European countries.

> **WEB SEARCH**
> www.sccfd.org/travel.html lists the emergency numbers for all countries

Your luggage

The golden rule is never to offer to carry someone else's luggage for them. But you also need to look after your own:

- keep your bags locked and in sight at all times
- never leave your luggage unattended
- put a distinctive marker on your luggage, including your backpack
- don't place money, documents or valuables in checked-in luggage
- if your luggage is lost or damaged, report it to the airline immediately and ask for a written report
- never discard your luggage receipt until you have safely claimed your bags from the carousel – and checked that they are yours
- if your luggage appears to have been tampered with, don't claim it from the carousel, report it
- don't hang back at the carousel – watch for your luggage to appear so that no-one else takes it

- consider writing your business address on the labels of your suitcase, rather than your home address. Otherwise, a luggage thief will not only know you are on holiday, but know where to find your empty house
- you're unlikely to have your suitcases beside you when travelling by train, so keep an eye on them when the train is at a station

TRAVEL TIP

If you are the victim of theft, report it to the police and ask for a written report to support an insurance claim.

Transport

Stay alert when you're taking public transport or taxis, or driving in unfamiliar cities:
- know (or ask) what an official taxi looks like
- don't take unofficial taxis
- don't share taxis with strangers
- leave a taxi door open while you retrieve your luggage from the boot and items from inside the vehicle, so that the driver can't drive off before you've checked that you have everything
- stay alert at transition points (for example, stepping off an escalator, boarding a train) – this is a time when a pickpocket will take advantage of your distraction
- when driving in a city, keep the windows up and doors locked
- the hire company sticker on your hire car signals *tourist* – never leave valuables in the car

Accommodation

In accommodation, as with other things, you usually get what you pay for. If it is very cheap, there are probably snags. Accommodation safety issues include:
- don't answer a knock at the door before verifying who the person is
- if you arrange to meet someone you don't know, meet in a public place (a cafe, a hotel lobby), not at your accommodation or hotel room

- keep the address of where you are staying with you when you go out sightseeing, so if you can't find your way back, you can hand the address to a taxi driver to deliver you there
- if staying in a multi-storey hotel, ask for a room a few floors up, so that you can open the window without fear of someone breaking into your room
- always take your accommodation keys with you when you go out

TRAVEL TIP

If you're planning to stay in hotels, take extra copies of the information page of your passport. When hotels request to hold your passport during your stay give them the photocopy. This means you don't lose sight of your passport, or pay an exorbitant hotel price for a photocopy.

Eating

Common sense will keep you healthy:
- if in any doubt, boil water before drinking
- always check the seal on a bottle of drink you have purchased
- when dining out, ask for bottles of wine or water to be opened at your table
- wash fruit and vegetables; if unsure, stick to thick-skinned fruit and vegetables that need peeling
- carry some soap leaves, tissues and antibacterial wipes in your day pack, to maintain personal hygiene while on the move
- when you cook food yourself, you know the ingredients are fresh, the preparation hygienic and the eating utensils clean

On the street

This is the place where you'll want to blend in to keep safe. A loud checked shirt, a camera around the neck, some flashy gold jewellery and an aimless walk are beacons to pickpockets. Also:
- keep all valuables out of sight in a money belt or neck pouch
- don't withdraw and carry too much cash
- stay alert, even when taking in the sights
- ask your host about safe and unsafe areas, especially if you're going to go out after dark

- check the credentials of a 'tour guide' who offers to show you the sights of a city
- as well as maps, consider a hand-held GPS to lessen the chance of getting lost
- at a cafe, loop a strap from your bag or backpack around the leg of the chair you're sitting on, and keep in contact with it between your feet
- learn some basic emergency services words from your phrasebook, even if they are limited to expressions of 'help' or 'police'
- if you are the victim of a theft, don't fight back
- don't forget to wear a hat and apply sunscreen during summer

Keep your money safe

Don't carry too much cash – if it's lost or stolen you have no proof of how much has gone. Also:

- before leaving home, clear your wallet of unnecessary credit and other cards
- divide cash and credit cards between you and your travel partner
- don't carry your wallet in your back pocket
- use a money belt
- if carrying a purse in a handbag or backpack, keep your money in a safe spot, keep your bag firmly closed, and carry it in a way that it is safe from theft (in a queue, always have your bag at your chest)
- don't leave cash lying around in your hotel room
- don't let your credit card out of sight in shops, restaurants and hotels
- keep an eye out when using ATMs – if there are two of you, one should be facing out from the machine, keeping watch
- use ATMs in daylight
- don't hang around at the ATM to count your money – move off to a safer place
- check the ATM before you use it for a scam where a small box is placed in front of the point where you insert your card. It's a device that reads the metallic strip on your

card, while a concealed camera records your PIN entry. Banks now check daily for this criminal use of ATMs
- if using a public computer to transfer funds or pay bills on the internet, make sure it has current anti-virus protection, that you log out completely when you finish, and that you erase the browser history of your use (in Internet Explorer: Tools > Internet Options > Clear History)
- use only reputable money exchange outlets to exchange money
- keep the traveller's cheques receipt separate from the cheques
- record the emergency numbers to call if your credit card is lost or stolen, as you will need to cancel it quickly

TRAVEL TIP
Safety and your camera:
- don't carry your camera in its brand-bearing case, conceal it in your backpack
- don't loop it over your shoulder
- don't loop it over the back of a chair in a cafe or sit it on the table
- don't hang it around your neck (one quick blade swipe will free it for a thief)
- when using your camera, wrap the strap a couple of times around your wrist
- download your images onto a laptop or portable digital storage device, or have them burnt onto a CD
- consider taking a disposable camera rather than an expensive one

KEEPING IN TOUCH

Like credit cards, mobile phones have changed the nature of travel. You can send photos to friends, book a taxi, check your flights, find your way around, transfer money and pay bills.

Before leaving home, set your phone up for global roaming (see Chapter 2) and enter all the numbers you'll need in your address book. For those at home you will be contacting, convert their number to the international dialling format. This makes it quick to call, and it also means your phone will recognise their incoming calls.

Keeping in regular touch with family and friends at home not only assures them of your safety, it will also alert them to mishap if they don't hear from you for some time. If you're going to be out of contact range, let someone know when they can next expect to hear from you – and keep the appointment. If you are travelling in an area where there is a civil emergency or other major incident (something that will be reported on world news), contact your family immediately to assure them of your safety.

You can easily clock up a large phone bill using your mobile phone overseas. Remember that when you're retrieving messages from your message bank, you are calling Australia. Local calls are at the local rate of the carrier you have logged into. You can check the rates of competing carriers before you leave home, so you know which one to select. Email and SMS are much cheaper ways of keeping in touch.

> **WEB SEARCH**
> See www.telstra.com.au > mobile > international roaming > select country to check carrier rates

Phone cards are the most inexpensive means of phoning home. They're usually cheaper to buy at your destination (up to one-third less) rather than at home. You'll usually find the best deals in the backpacker area of a city, and most post offices and tourism information centres sell them. The downside is the need to use landlines, which are becoming increasingly rare unless you're staying in a hotel.

If you're not taking your own means of sending emails, internet cafes are now everywhere. For a congenial internet setting, hunt out the local library – some of the backpacker internet cafes are more than seedy. Other places where you'll find public internet access include banks, post offices, hotels, department stores and airports.

> **WEB SEARCH**
> For a worldwide list of internet cafes, see www.cybercafes.com.
> If using your own computer, you can access a list of wi-fi hotspots around the world at www.jiwire.com

It's possible to set up your own website and record through text and photos the progress of your travels for all the world to share (or at least those in the world who are interested in knowing what you're up to).

> **WEB SEARCH**
> Travel diary websites include www.travelpod.com and www.getjealous.com

Postcards might be old technology, but for the receiver they still mean that you've gone to some trouble to keep in touch (even if the postcard does arrive weeks after you return home). They're more evocative than an SMS, and more colourful to keep.

TRAVEL TIP
To make it easy to send postcards, and avoid the risk of forgetting someone, prepare printed mailing labels before leaving home. Then, you don't even need to take an address book.

CONSULAR SERVICES

The Australian government has a network of consular offices, embassies and high commissions throughout the world, although not in every country. If you find yourself in trouble, these are the places to seek help. Before leaving home, research the contact details for the consular offices in the countries you will be visiting, and record their addresses and phone numbers. You can find this information on **www.smartraveller.gov.au**. In addition to the overseas offices, the Department of Foreign Affairs and

Trade (DFAT) operates a twenty-four-hour emergency phone in Canberra that you can contact for assistance from anywhere in the world. There are two numbers: +61 2 6261 3305, or +61 1300 555 135.

While consular assistance is available for a range of issues, it cannot override local laws, even if those laws don't make sense to you. To find out about local laws, visit the DFAT website and check for each relevant country.

CHECKLIST

Enter the following emergency numbers in your mobile phone, and also make a hardcopy list.

- ❏ the relevant consular offices
- ❏ the DFAT emergency number in Canberra
- ❏ your travel insurance company
- ❏ relevant countries' emergency numbers
- ❏ your ICE numbers

Death overseas

Death through illness or accident is part of the reality of travel and it is simply good planning to know in advance what to do if this happens to someone you're travelling with.

Before you leave home, check that your travel insurance covers the cost of an overseas funeral, or for the return of remains to Australia.

Overseas, if your travelling companion dies, you should turn to the consular service for help. They can assist with notifying family at home, providing a list of local funeral directors and lawyers if needed, registering the death, managing the media, and giving advice on transporting the remains home.

Contact your insurance company immediately. Many insurance companies go beyond just financial cover to give considerable advice and assistance in making the necessary arrangements.

TIME OUT

It's odd that so many people subject themselves to more rush, stress and exhaustion while travelling than they would ever tolerate at home. It's because you're trying to make the most of your precious holiday, but time out – quiet moments for reflection – should be built into your itinerary, for self-preservation and for relaxation. You don't want to return home so tired that you feel disappointed by your experience.

Out on the sightseeing trail, you can find free retreats in public parks and gardens, public libraries, churches and the lobbies of large hotels. For the price of a coffee, you can sit at a pavement cafe for ages, watching the passing parade.

TRAVEL TIP
A tip about toilets: always carry some loose change, tissues and antibacterial wipes. Department stores often have the cleanest toilets.

Think of your accommodation not just as a place to eat and sleep, but as a place to plan your day over a leisurely breakfast, and review all you've experienced over a pre-dinner drink. Use your accommodation for reading, or become truly culturally attuned by adopting the European habit of an afternoon siesta.

Plan your travels so that it's not all city-based. Build in some quiet retreats in the countryside or by the ocean, and use these times for simpler pleasures such as long walks and leisurely picnics.

TRAVEL TIP
Waiting is an unavoidable part of the travel experience. Plan in advance how you will fill these moments so they're not wasted:
- crosswords and sudoku
- writing a journal
- writing postcards
- reading about the place you're visiting (going beyond a guidebook)
- learning the language from your phrasebook
- testing your language skills on all the advertising that surrounds you, or with a local newspaper

THERE'S MORE TO TRAVEL THAN SHOPPING

In most tourism industry surveys asking people about their motivations for travel, shopping appears high on the list. Why is this? It's as if the world has become one large shopping mall, as if consuming equates to entertainment, as if as tourists we can come to understand a foreign culture by visiting the High Street shops. The reality is that High Streets are almost the same everywhere: same global brands, same merchandise, same profit motivation. Shops are the most telling symptom of the homogenisation of the world. Travelling through Germany, I had decided that the one item I would buy myself was a pair of spectacle frames (the Germans wear fabulous glasses). I purchased a pair that I thought were sufficiently different that I would not be able to find them in Australia. Some months later, I met a friend who was wearing the identical frames. Where did she buy them? I expected her to say Frankfurt, but no, Bentleigh!

Souvenir shops are special traps. In any country or city, it's very much a case of 'seen one, seen them all'. While they claim to sell items that represent the local culture, they're usually clichés of a past that only vaguely connect with the place. Think of all those shamrocks in Ireland, sombreros in Spain, tartan in Scotland, or trolls in Norway. These are usually topped up with fridge magnets, tea towels, flags, gaudy coffee mugs and stuffed toys, most of which are unlikely to have been made locally.

The problem with shopping is that it's generally a hollow exercise. Appearing to be interesting and fun at the time, you finish your day with the nagging feeling that the time has been wasted and you have nothing of intrinsic or personal value to show for your efforts. You can shop at home; save your travel time to spend on the experiences that will reveal difference and understanding.

There are exceptions. There may be some local craft or cultural items that are famous, such as glass from Murano, or amber from Copenhagen. Or there may be something that you have seen on your walks that has special significance. These are things that you usually find in non-touristy shops in back streets. We have a Norwegian flagpole finial in our Metung backyard.

They're on all the flagpoles in that country, and we found one in a jumbled, dusty shop selling maritime objects.

Before you buy a souvenir, take a moment to consider what you're going to do with it at home. If you can bring it into everyday use, then it has real value as a memento.

TRAVEL TIP
For a completely different 'souvenir', think about taking a language, cooking, history or other course during your travels. That way you come home with new knowledge and a lifelong memory.

SHOPPING GREEN

Here's a challenge: plan to travel without shopping beyond the necessities. After all, consumerism is one of the underlying contributors to global warming.

Other responsible shopping approaches can include the following:
- buy local; in this way you are supporting the local community, and the goods haven't been flown in
- shop at small businesses, rather than multinational stores
- say no to wrappings and bags that you know you'll leave behind because you don't need them in your suitcase; use your recycle bag or backpack instead
- don't buy anything from a threatened species, or threatened natural resource
- don't buy pirated CDs and DVDs – they're illegal, and the quality is usually so bad that no matter what you pay, you've wasted your money
- don't buy copy products (watches, handbags) – they're usually trash, preying on the consumer's belief that brand is more important than either use or quality

9

FOOD, HEALTH AND FITNESS

*If you reject the food, ignore the customs,
fear the religion and avoid the people,
you might better stay at home.*

James Michener

- An appetite for travel
- Good food – it's in your hands
- Eating green
- Fit to travel
- Jet lag and DVT
- Pilates for planes and other places
- Incidental exercise
- Avoiding the museum shuffle
- Exercises for tight spaces

AN APPETITE FOR TRAVEL

No matter where you travel – to a neighbouring town or the other side of the world – food forms a focus of your journey, partly because it is a fundamental necessity, but it's also an accessible route into the culture of a place. Of all the foreignness you can experience, food is the most obvious. Of all the challenges to your prejudices and set ways, food is the one you are most likely to confront. If you're a foodie, it's one of the most pleasurable aspects of travelling.

There are so many ways to consume local produce: from shopping at village markets to visiting farms, dining in cafes with spectacular views, and browsing the supermarket shelves and musing over the foreign-looking ingredients.

For me, the joy of self-contained accommodation is the

opportunity to purchase fresh produce and prepare meals. On our first visit to Paris we stayed in a lovely hotel, but without any cooking facilities. Daily we visited the local supermarket where the delicatessen section was nothing less than spectacular. We roamed past the fishmongers with their catch spread out on pavement tables, we longed for a reason to buy the huge globe artichokes piled up in wooden crates outside small shops – I could taste the leaves drenched in olive oil and garlic. But all to no avail. We ate in cafes and restaurants that were excellent, and bought from glorious patisseries, but felt that we were only exposing ourselves to part of the experience; we were missing a sense of the exotic that beckoned from all the fresh produce on display on the streets. (We also missed buying from the *boucheries chevalines*!)

Years later, having learned the lesson, we were staying in a small farmhouse in the Dordogne, and on a blue and balmy late-summer afternoon we visited the local trout farm. A two-storey timber farmhouse nestled among birch, walnut and chestnut trees showing just a hint of autumn colour. Intensely green lawns dipped down to a broad stream. An elderly woman answered our knock on the door, appearing in gumboots and stockings that didn't quite meet the hem of her woollen skirt. She draped a fishing net across her shoulder, and took us to the bank of the stream, asking us what size trout we wanted.

Here she watched the water for a few moments, seeing through the sparkles that caught the ruffled surface of the fast-moving stream, then cast out the net so that it opened and fanned over the surface. With a deft tug, the net enclosed three glistening fish and she hauled the catch to shore. She swapped the fish for a few euros. That evening, in the cooling air on the terrace of 'our' house, we enjoyed one of the best meals of our lives. As we ate, five brightly coloured air balloons rose up from the valley below, and drifted across the evening sky towards the mountains – the perfect accompaniment.

For me, buying ingredients for a meal is as much a part of the travel experience and a chance to understand a culture as visiting a museum. I love the sense of feeling like a local as I scan the supermarket shelves or compare the prices of tomatoes at a market. It becomes a daily event – a very European habit – and it is another activity that separates the holiday experience from the everyday at home. If you're not sure about an ingredient, what it is and how it's cooked – ask (even if it does ruin the image of your looking like a local), otherwise you might be missing a local delicacy. Your host at the property where you're staying can be a good source of information about local foods and how to prepare them. So can fellow shoppers.

TRAVEL TIP

- if you're carrying food, make sure it is in lightweight containers (not glass or cans); decant if necessary into plastic bags
- to seal bags of rice, cereal etc use those long plastic clips sold by Ikea, or zip-lock plastic bags
- a lightweight plastic food box with a firmly fitting lid is ideal for picnic lunches, or to safely carry ingredients in your luggage
- a sharp knife is useful; a corkscrew indispensable
- take fabric shopping bags, as most European supermarkets don't offer plastic carry bags unless you pay for them. You can use the bags for all sorts of things, and you're doing the environment a favour
- buy colourful serviettes and a candle to make any table setting look inviting

Still, cafes can be a great introduction to what the locals eat – provided you avoid the obvious tourist traps. It's worth watching where the locals go to eat, as it's likely to be both authentic and affordable. It won't always be the obvious places that give you the best experience.

One evening in Sicily, we walked along the foreshore at Naxos, looking for a place to eat. This fairly seedy fishing town is at the base of the cliff that supports all the beauty and wealth of Taormina, with its views across the Mediterranean and towards Mount Etna. We decided on pizza at a cafe that appeared to have a lot of locals dining at the outdoor tables. They turned out to be members of the family. When we ordered our pizzas, a bulky women went to a Fiat parked nearby and banged loudly on the passenger door. A scruffy, skinny man unfolded his sleepy form and disappeared into the kitchen. This was not looking good.

But a beautiful pottery jug of ordinary but drinkable red wine was placed on our table, and the pizzas, when they arrived, were delicious. We sat looking across the beach strewn with timber fishing boats, to the gently lapping ocean beyond.

All of this is to say that your holiday can be a mix of eating experiences, requiring only an open mind and a love of good food.

TRAVEL TIP
Eating out can break the budget, but there are some ways of making it economical:
- look to see where the locals are eating
- ask your hosts where they eat, where they recommend
- guidebook recommendations can be out of date, so check these with your host
- seek out ethnic quarters in big cities – the food is usually a bit cheaper
- cooked breakfasts can be a weight on your wallet
- when all else fails, a pizza is reliable, filling and cheap, and available almost anywhere
- avoid fast foods, they're similarly unappetising the world over
- eat with the goal of not putting on weight during your holiday

GOOD FOOD – IT'S IN YOUR HANDS

Cooking is not just fun; it also makes travelling far more affordable. Breakfast can be leisurely as you start your day, lunch a picnic in a beautiful setting, and dinner a delight from the market you have visited.

WEB SEARCH
Visit the websites of the country towns you will be visiting to check which days the regional markets operate, eg for farmers markets in the UK, see
www.farmersmarkets.net

CHECKLIST

You need only a few basics for preparing glorious meals. For example:

- olive oil
- good coffee, and a small bialetti to make it
- teabags of your favourite brew
- vegemite (yes, a cliché for Australians, but it must be popular as it is now produced in travel tubes)
- garlic
- sea salt, ground pepper and your favourite dried herbs and spices (pack in tiny plastic bags like those used by jewellers)

After that, shopping daily makes planning a menu easy.

Breakfast

Of all the meals, breakfast is the one where tradition dies slowly, and where our accepted notions of a meal can be most challenged. Being faced with pickled herring or liver pate at 8 a.m. may not be your normal experience, but it is one that reminds you that you have travelled far from home. Sometimes it's just the tourist special, such as kippers in Scotland, but it can still be a difference to be savoured. Even if you are preparing breakfast in your accommodation, add the colour of the local cuisine.

The breakfast traditions of some countries are superb. Standing up at a bar in France or Italy with dolci and cappuccino, surrounded by locals greeting each other, reading newspapers and swapping gossip, is my idea of breakfast heaven overseas. (Although Fred complains ten minutes later that he needs a 'real' breakfast.)

TRAVEL TIP

It's not only de rigueur to drink your cappuccino standing up at a bar in France and Italy; you'll be charged more for your coffee if you sit at a table.

Lunch

Whether you're taking time out for lunch or keeping on the go, eat well to maintain your energy levels through the afternoon.

- a cafe stop in the middle of the day lets you sit for a while (use the toilet) and watch the passing parade; it's also usually a cheaper meal than in the evening
- picnic lunches are great – they provide a break in your day, and you can settle down on a park bench or a rock by the ocean and take in the scene around you. It need only be as simple as good bread, a chunk of cheese, a salami and fresh fruit, but do try to make sure the ingredients are the local specialties
- packets of dried fruit and nuts are worth keeping in your backpack as a good source of nourishment if you don't want to pause in your sightseeing

Dinner

The suggestions given following are mostly of a Mediterranean style because these are the dishes most easily prepared while you're travelling: fresh ingredients which are readily available almost everywhere, especially in markets, and without reliance on a well-stocked pantry. Do find out about and cook the local specialties wherever possible.

TRAVEL TIP
Why not do some research first about the local cuisines, and photocopy some recipes to take with you?

Bruschetta: fresh ciabatta grilled and topped with chopped tomatoes, red onion, garlic and a drizzle of olive oil

Antipasto: the cheese of the country you're in (small handmade goats cheese, salty fetta), olives, prosciutto, salami and glorious fresh bread

Pasta: with a sauce of fresh tomatoes and herbs; with local seafood mix, in a sauce of butter and cream and lots of black pepper; have some parmesan cheese on hand for topping pasta (also good for serving with pre-dinner drinks)

Risotto: with any fresh green vegetable – asparagus, beans, peas – just add some garlic, white wine and stock, and top with parmesan cheese

Salads: seared salmon broken into chunks and mixed through salad greens, with a lemony dressing; crispy fried chorizo sausage with salad greens, grilled tomatoes and bocconcini; grilled haloumi with greens, olives, tomatoes; pan-fried squid or octopus with rocket and lemon wedges

Something special: duck or a plump yellow chicken from a regional market, roasted with lots of vegetables; local seafood (make sure it's fresh), pan fried with a fresh herb sauce

Dessert

After you've finished your main course, go for an evening stroll, buy a gelato and sit down to watch the evening parade as the locals bring their day to an end. In Britain, a local pub will beckon for a nightcap, and of course, if you're in Belgium, the chocolate is a splendid end to a meal. Fresh fruit is not only a good option, but a must in your diet while you're travelling.

TRAVEL TIP

If you have any doubt about the water quality, boil it before drinking (boil it the night before, and put it into your water bottles the next morning), or drink purchased bottled water.

If you succumb to travellers' diarrhoea, drink small amounts of clear fluid often, eat simple carbohydrate foods, and rest. If the diarrhoea persists, talk to a pharmacist about rehydration products, or seek medical attention.

EATING GREEN

I don't just mean eat your veggies; there are many choices you can make that help the environment and local communities.
- use a recyclable shopping bag
- buy organic food wherever possible
- buy food with the least amount of packaging
- buy fresh from farmers markets
- buy locally produced food – food that hasn't had to be flown in

FIT TO TRAVEL

The flip side to eating all this delicious food is ensuring you don't pile on the pounds. You don't want your most enduring holiday memento to be a tyre around your waist. Exercise at home has much to do with routine – you build it into your daily or weekly schedule and it's not such a task. But remove that schedule and somehow it becomes difficult to even remember to exercise, let alone be motivated enough to do it.

Once again, planning is important. To start, you need to be fit and healthy before you leave home. This might include a medical check-up some weeks before your departure date, and it should include a determination to be fit and energetic for your travels. Consider joining a gym at least three months in advance to establish a base fitness level.

TRAVEL TIP
- there are medical clinics that specialise in travellers' needs, from vaccinations to medical check-ups
- pack a first-aid kit
- don't forget to include a dental check-up in your holiday preparations
- if you wear spectacles, have an eye test and take with you both a spare pair of glasses and your current prescription

WEB SEARCH
For clinics that specialise in travel-related medicine, see www.travelclinic.com.au or www.traveldoctor.com.au
At www.traveldoctor.com.au you can buy a first-aid kit tailored to the type of travel you plan to do

Well before you go, put on those new walkers you've bought for your trip and hit the road. You'll be doing a lot of walking while you're away, so you'll want to ensure that your shoes are comfortable and that you take the exercise in your stride. Plan to walk for at least thirty minutes three times a week. Use the time to dream about your holiday, and keep in mind how you are boosting your energy levels for your time away.

Draw up an exercise program that you think you can stick to while travelling, and rehearse it before you leave. The biggest hurdle to exercising is getting started, so doing this before you leave home will establish a pattern that you can more easily fall into. And you can't use the excuse that you're not sure what to do.

TRAVEL TIP
- draw up a workout routine before leaving home – ask your gym trainer to create one for you or make up a routine from the exercises and spreadsheet given later in this chapter
- build exercise into your holiday routine, just as you'd include it in your everyday routine

JET LAG AND DVT

Every traveller should be aware of the symptoms and treatments that are available to avoid jet lag and DVT.

Jet lag
Jet lag is always an issue on long flights that cross time zones, upsetting the body's time clock and disrupting eating and sleeping patterns. Travelling east (usually the return direction from Europe to Australia) is more disruptive to your system because you are moving forward in time. From London to Sydney, you travel through nine time zones, and the recovery time is normally calculated as one day to recover for each time zone crossed. This is a fairly generous period; for some people it only takes a day or two to overcome the effects.

> **WEB SEARCH**
> To check the time differences between departure point and destination, see
> www.timeanddate.com/worldclock/converter.html

Jet lag symptoms can include fatigue, irritability and anxiety, which is not a good way to feel at the beginning of a holiday. Constipation and dehydration can also be a problem (another reason to drink plenty of water during the flight). But it's not all bad: I love the experience of waking very early to a European summer morning, to the surreal pearly grey dawn that is so different from that at home.

TRAVEL TIP
To help reduce the effects of jet lag:
- drink plenty of water during the flight, and limit alcohol and caffeine
- if possible, take a flight that arrives at your destination in the evening, so that you can go to bed and help reset your biological time clock
- get out in the sunshine and trick your body into knowing when it's daytime
- exercise to keep alert, and to tire your body for a good night's sleep
- if you're on medication, adjust it to local time in a way that you don't skip a dose
- don't compare times – live in the local time zone without thinking, 'This is really 2 a.m. and I should be in bed'
- eat the correct meal for the local time zone

DVT

Deep vein thrombosis (DVT) is commonly known as economy class syndrome because it's the cramped quarters that you are confined to for long hours without movement that can contribute to the problem. Other contributing factors are the lower air pressure and oxygen levels, and the drier air in the aircraft cabin.

DVT symptoms are a swollen or painful leg, especially the calf, and/or breathing difficulties. Report to a doctor immediately if you suffer from these symptoms, even up to a month after your flight.

TRAVEL TIP
- if you have a pre-existing condition (especially heart or vascular disease) see your doctor before travelling
- watch the in-flight documentary on exercises to do to avoid deep vein thrombosis, and do the exercises regularly throughout the flight
- drink plenty of water: what's offered and from the water bottle you brought with you. Drink one glass of water for every hour of flight
- get out of your seat every hour or two and walk the length of the plane

- do some stretching exercises while waiting in the toilet queue (see below)
- avoid tight clothing
- avoid sleeping tablets (they reduce your mobility)
- use the footrests provided at your seat
- ask your pharmacist or doctor about compression stockings
- spend in-transit time walking as fast as you can, and stretching (some airports have gyms and/or swimming pools)

PILATES FOR PLANES AND OTHER PLACES

Pilates is a series of exercises that build core strength, working on the deep internal muscles that assist with posture and ease of movement. They are good exercises for travelling as they require no equipment, you need only minimal space (some can be done sitting down), and the breathing routine that is an integral part of Pilates aids relaxation. You will need to become familiar with the exercises before you leave home, then you can do them anywhere without needing notes.

My thanks to Wendy Aitken at the YMCA in Lakes Entrance, who created a travel workout schedule for us some time ago, which has proved to be both challenging and achievable. All the exercises below are from Wendy.

The first step is to locate your deep abdominal muscles:

- stand up straight, feet shoulder width apart and your weight spread evenly on all parts of your feet (the ball, the heel and the side)
- place your palms on your abdomen and concentrate on drawing in the muscles behind your pelvis (think of a string at your back pulling the muscles in)
- don't tighten the muscles in your bottom to achieve the deep muscle contraction
- stand tall by separating your ribs from your hips, and rolling your shoulders up and back
- think of a string through the top of your head, pulling you taller
- rest your chin on the horizon

Now for the breathing:

- breathe in deeply through your nose, expanding your rib cage out sideways, not forwards
- breathe out through a loose, open mouth (making a 'hush' sound with your breath)
- make sure your don't lose the abdominal muscle contraction while breathing (or at any time during your workout)

Pilates rolldown

This basic Pilates move is wonderful for releasing your back at any time, but especially during a long flight:

- standing in the Pilates position described above, breathe in deeply
- drop your chin and breathe out as you slowly curve your spine, one vertebrae at a time, to roll down until your fingers touch your toes and you are looking through your legs
- at the bottom of the move take a deep breath in, ensure your abdominals are engaged and as you breathe out, let those muscles pull you up into the starting position
- at the top, roll your shoulders back and down to ensure an open chest and good posture
- repeat four times

TRAVEL TIP

Protect your back during your holiday:

- routinely swap your suitcase from one hand to the other (whether you're pulling or carrying)
- when lifting your heavy suitcase, bend your knees and engage your abdominal muscles to support your lower back
- use both shoulder straps of your backpack rather than slinging it over one shoulder
- when carrying heavy grocery bags, balance the weight evenly for each hand

In-your-seat exercises

Neck rolls
- breathe in and turn your head to your left shoulder
- as you breathe out, roll your chin down in an arc to your right shoulder
- repeat, side to side, four times

Alternate arm reaches
- keep shoulders back and down and chin neutral on the horizon
- stretch both arms long above your head
- reach higher with your left arm and release, reach higher with your right arm and release
- repeat eight times (explain to the crew that you're not trying to reach for the call button)

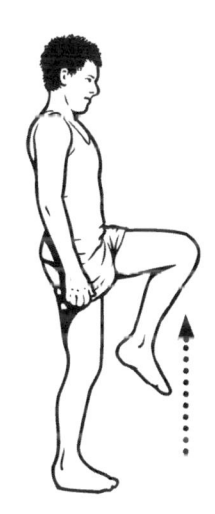

Alternate knee lifts
- engage your abdominal muscles
- lift your left leg to ninety degrees, lower leg to the floor
- lift your right leg to ninety degrees, lower leg to the floor
- repeat eight to twelve times

Alternate knee lifts with upper-body rotation
- follow the steps for alternate knee lifts
- when raising your left knee, rest your right hand behind your head and rotate your upper body as you lift your knee (repeat for right knee raise)
- repeat eight to twelve times

Knee squeezes
- place something soft between your knees and squeeze, holding the contraction for five counts, then release
- repeat four times

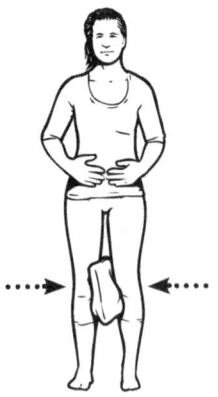

Exercises in transit

If you can find a quiet corner, do some upper-body moves. They'll release your spine and muscles and prepare you for sleeping through the second leg of your flight:

- start with a Pilates rolldown
- standing up straight with arms at shoulder height and elbows bent so your hands are in front of your chest, pull back twice, then pull back once with arms wide
- standing up straight with arms at your side and feet shoulder width apart, lean to the left and slide your hand down towards your knee, repeat for your right side

- stretch your quad muscles by lifting your knee and grasping your foot behind, just below your bottom, keep knees together and raise your free arm above your head for balance (or use a wall for balance)
- bend down on one knee, with the other leg out to the side, toe raised, to stretch your muscles, repeat for other side
- stand up straight with hands on hips, left leg forward with knee bent, right leg back, pushing your heel towards the floor, repeat for other side
- do some on-the-spot jogging, or walk briskly around the transit area
- raise the intensity of your walking by pumping your arms and taking longer strides

Pilates for sightseers

These moves are good to relieve your back after walking long distances on hard surfaces or up and down steep hills:

Child's pose stretch
On the floor, on your hands and knees, sink your bottom back to your heels and your chest towards the floor, reaching your arms long in front, take deep breathes in and out

Rest position
On the floor on your back, grasp your knees to your chest and gently lift your tailbone off the floor. To massage your spine, put your hands on your knees and make small circles with your knees clockwise, then anticlockwise.

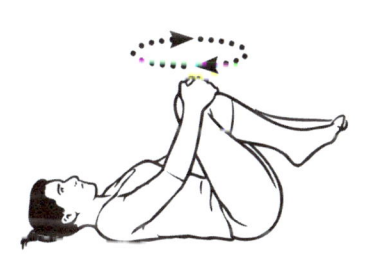

Cat stretch
On your hands and knees, drop your chin to your chest and pull your tailbone under so your back is arched and shoulders rounded, then reverse the stretch by pushing your chin forward and tailbone back so that you have a dip in your spine.

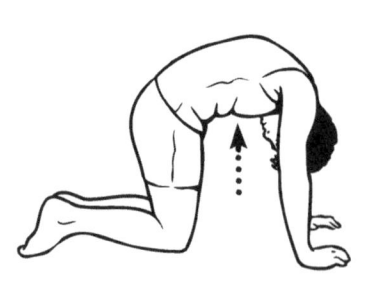

Lower-back rotation
- on the floor on your back, bend your knees to ninety degrees and raise your feet so you can see them above your knees; place your arms wide out at shoulder level
- breathe in, and as your breathe out drop your knees to one side without raising your shoulder off the floor 
- breathe in as you return your knees to the middle
- breathe out as you drop them to the other side

Rolling like a ball
- sit on the floor and draw your knees in to your chest, clasp the inside of your lower legs just above your ankles with your hands 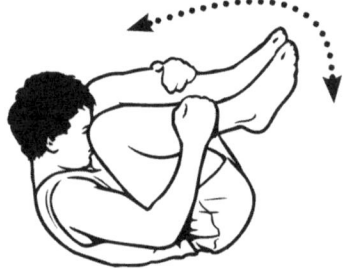
- round your spine by pulling in your abdomen and dropping your chin to your chest (your back needs to be well rounded to roll backwards and forwards)

- breathe in and push to roll onto your back and shoulders
- breathe out as your roll back up into the starting position
- stop before your toes touch the floor

INCIDENTAL EXERCISE

Incidental exercise takes in all those opportunities to build fitness without really trying. It's perfect for travelling as you don't need to visit a gym or pack heavy equipment, or even motivate yourself for an exercise routine.

Choosing to use public transport rather than hiring a car is not only good for the environment, it's good for you, too, as you'll be forced to walk more. It's the perfect travel pace: it slows you down so you can take in all that is around you. You'll never notice the gardens, the birdlife, the small architectural motifs that make up a place when you're zooming by in a car.

Strolling wears you out more quickly than walking briskly. They say you can wear out a cat by making it walk slowly. Having a purposeful stride is also safer as you won't be so easily marked out by pickpockets as a tourist. So be conscious of your pace.

Whenever you stop to look at something, be aware of your posture: draw in your deep abdominal muscles, roll your shoulders back and down, and stand a little taller (as described for the Pilates rolldown exercise).

It's a holiday, so think of taking in such holiday activities as golf, tennis, swimming, skiing and sailing. Pack your bathers in case you stay at a hotel with a pool; but for other activities, simply hire the gear there.

Cycling is good exercise, and more and more cities are now providing bikes for tourist transport. But if you haven't ridden for years, beware. It might be that you never lose the skill, but you do lose the muscles. We once hired bikes at Aldebrough, in the south-west of England, to cycle to Snape Maltings. The next day we were in agony: every muscle ached, and we were so saddle-sore we looked ridiculous when we walked. So if you plan to cycle, practise – and toughen up – before leaving home.

WORKOUT ROUTINE (example)

Use this form to create your own exercise routine for travelling.

EXERCISE DESCRIPTION	REPEATS	
Warm-up jog on spot		5 min
Pilates rolldown		3
R-8 Arnold press		8
R-8 lateral pull-down		8
R-8 tricep extension		8
R-8 bicep curl		8
Push-ups		20
R-8 standing side bends		8
R-8 front raise		8
R-8 side raise		8
R-8 upright row		8
Squats		20
Dips		15
R-8 chest expansion		8
R-8 single arm row and squat		8
R-8 standing side leg lift		8
R-8 standing straight leg extension		8
Hovers		1 min
Crunches		30
Lower-back rotation		2
Cat stretch		2
Pilates rolldown		2

DATES									
1	2	3	4	5	6	7	8	9	10

TRAVEL TIP
- walking on sand is good exercise
- city parks and gardens are there for enjoyment and fitness
- explore national parks – for their beauty and your health
- at airports, shun the conveyor belt and walk instead
- always take to the stairs rather than using escalators or lifts
- hide remote controls and get out of your seat
- get lost: lose yourself walking in the alleyways and back streets of old towns and cities
- care for your feet (they're a vital travel tool). Peppermint lotion is good for soothing tired feet, and pack some small sponge pads for relieving sore heels or toes
- smelly joggers are a packing problem. Pack them in an outside pocket of your suitcase, swamp them in bicarbonate soda, put them in a plastic bag and freeze overnight, or leave them at home

AVOIDING THE MUSEUM SHUFFLE

The pace at museums is not good for fitness. All that shuffling from one exhibit to the next, and standing for long periods, is very tiring and often leads to what I think of as 'museum back' – that dull ache in the lower back. There are a few simple ways to avoid the problem:

- don't spend too long in a museum – better to plan to return the next day than spend too many hours at an uncomfortable pace
- walk briskly between exhibits
- roll your shoulders to release the tension in your neck and shoulders
- rock onto your toes and back onto your heels, and bend your knees into small squats, to relieve your legs
- practise simple isometrics – clench your abdominal muscles and arch your back
- find a quiet corner and do a few Pilates rolldowns to release the tension in your back, and some quad stretches for your legs

Later, when you return to your accommodation, if your back is still aching, try the exercises in the section 'Pilates for sightseers'.

EXERCISES FOR TIGHT SPACES

You don't need a gym full of intricate equipment to exercise (although keep in mind most hotel gyms are nearly always deserted). Two simple and lightweight devices for travelling are a skipping rope and Resistance-8 cables.

Skipping is a high calorie burner and excellent cardio exercise, but it does have its drawbacks. It's not always socially acceptable – either on a crowded street or in your hotel room where the thumping can drive other guests crazy and you need to watch the light fittings and ornaments. But if you have the space – staying in a house with a yard, or a park – then it's good value. You don't even really need a skipping rope: going through the motions is sufficient for exercise. If you haven't skipped for years, you'll be surprised how hard it is to even reach twenty skips. For a good workout, skip for 100 to 200 rotations, rest for one minute, then repeat four to ten times.

Resistance-8 cables (or Power-8s) consist of two interlinked rubber tubes that provide a good substitute for weights. They allow you to do weight-bearing, muscle-toning exercises, using your body as the anchor for stretching the bands. They are lightweight and portable and come in a variety of resistances depending on your strength.

The following workouts can be easily managed in tight spaces and will exercise both upper and lower body.

Arnold press (sitting or standing)
- hold a grip of the Resistance-8 (R8) in each hand, arms at shoulder height, elbows at ninety degrees, palms towards your face
- reach arms up
- open arms wide above head (resistance)
- pull band down to chin
- return to the start position
- repeat eight to twelve times

Lateral pulldown front and back (sitting or standing)
- hold a grip of the R8 in each hand, extend arms above head
- stretch wide (resistance)
- bend elbows to bring the R8 back to chin level
- extend arms above head again, but bring the R8 down behind your neck
- repeat eight to twelve times

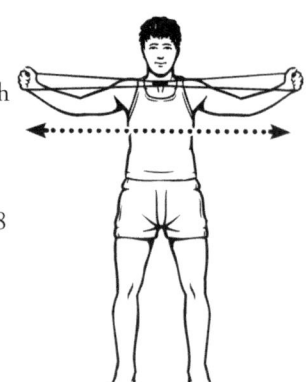

Tricep extension (sitting or standing)
- place left hand on right shoulder, holding both rings of the R8
- right hand holds one ring in an overhand grip
- extend the right hand down the side of your body, hinging at the elbow and keeping the upper arm still (resistance)
- repeat for both arms eight to twelve times

Bicep curl (sitting or standing)
- loop one ring of the R8 under your left foot, holding the other loop in an under-hand grip in your left hand
- curl your left arm up to your shoulder (resistance)
- repeat for both arms eight to twelve times

FOOD, HEALTH AND FITNESS

Seated knee open and close
- step inside either a single or double loop of the R8, placing it just under your knee joint
- open and close your knees (resistance)
- repeat eight times

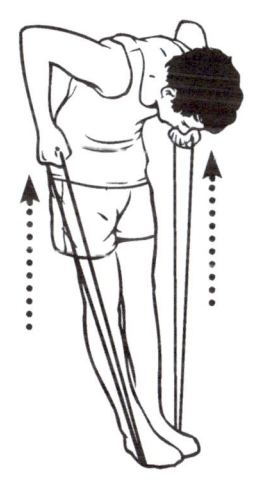

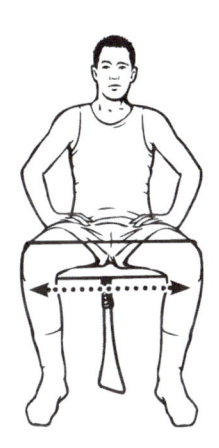

Bent-over row (sitting or standing)
- hold a grip of the R8 in each hand, looping the R8 under your feet
- lean forward over your knees and draw your elbows back, squeezing through the shoulder blades
- release and repeat eight to twelve times

Standing side bends
- loop one ring of the R8 under your right foot, hold the other in your right hand
- start with your arm resting by your side, bend the elbow and draw your hand up the side of your body, leaning to the opposite side (resistance)
- release and repeat each side eight times

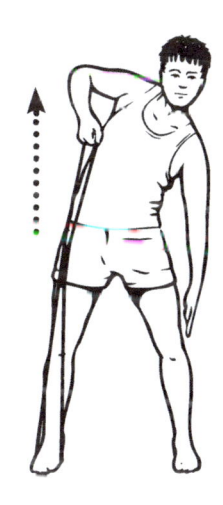

190 THE INTELLIGENT TRAVELLER

Standing front raise
- loop one ring of the R8 under your right foot and hold the other in your right hand
- rest your right hand on the front of your right leg, then extend your arm in front to shoulder height, keeping a slightly bent elbow
- repeat both sides eight to twelve times

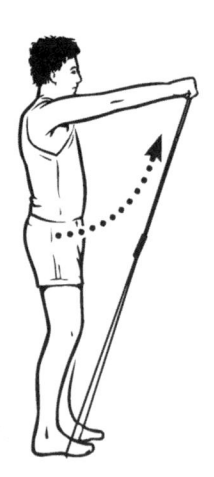

Standing side raise
- as before, but rest your hand on the side of your leg and extend your arms outwards to shoulder height, keeping a slightly bent elbow
- repeat both sides eight to twelve times

Upright row
- loop one ring of the R8 under both feet, hold the other ring with both hands
- bend elbows and lift hands to chest height
- repeat eight to twelve times

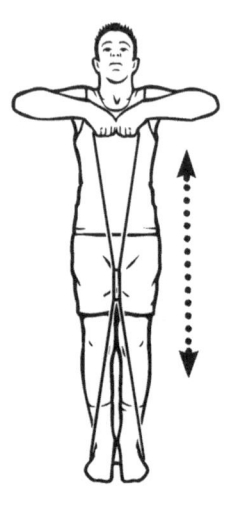

Chest expansion
- hold a grip of the R8 in each hand, arms extended in front and at shoulder height, palms facing each other
- open and close arms to expand and contract your chest
- repeat eight times

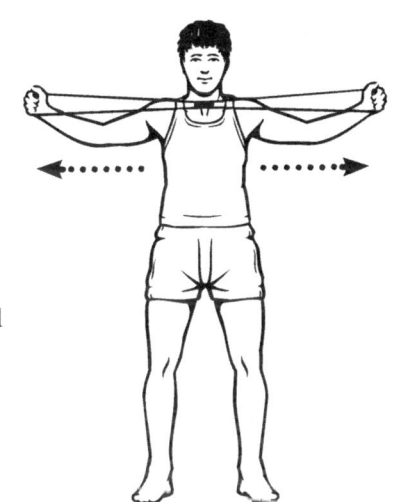

Single arm row and squat
- loop one ring of the R8 under your right foot, hold the other in your left hand
- rest your left hand on your right thigh
- keeping your hand close to your body, bend the left elbow to draw the band across your chest
- as your draw your elbow up, sit back in a squat (your abdominal muscles need to be engaged or your chest will drop forward)
- repeat both sides eight to twelve times

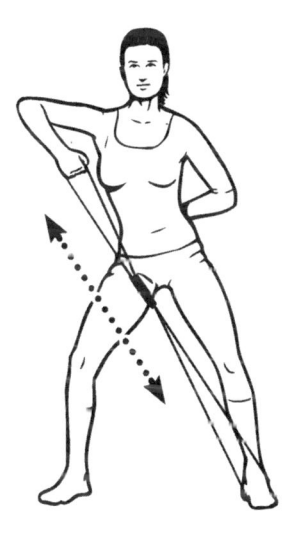

192 THE INTELLIGENT TRAVELLER

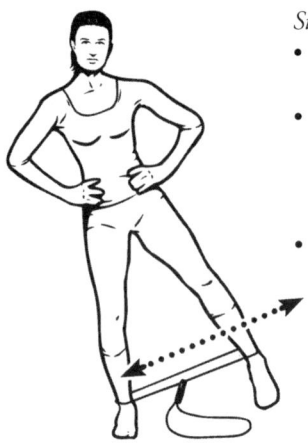

Standing side leg lift
- loop one or both rings of the R8 just above your ankles
- brace your abdominal muscles and extend your left leg out to the side, keeping your knees soft
- repeat both sides eight times

Standing straight leg extension
- as above but extend your leg behind, squeezing through your abdominals, bottom and hamstring muscles
- repeat both sides eight times

Following are more exercises that can be done in tight spaces without equipment. Remember to do some low-intensity warm-up and cool-down exercises with each routine, for example jog on the spot, or do step-ups for five minutes.

Push-ups
On the floor, on your knees or your toes, hands shoulder width or wider apart and looking forward of your hands to protect your neck, bend your elbows to lower your body towards the floor. Remember that you can do push-ups standing up against a wall, for an easy, do-anywhere exercise. Repeat twenty times.

Crunches
On the floor, on your back with elbows bent and hands just behind your ears, feet flat to the floor with knees bent (or knees bent and legs raised), use your abdominal muscles (not your neck) to draw yourself up. Repeat twenty times.

Hovers
Face down on the floor, on your knees or your toes, and on your elbows, looking forward of your hands, raise your abdomen and keep it raised and tight. Hold for one minute.

Side hovers
On the floor, on your side, rest with your hand or forearm on the floor, with your wrist or elbow directly under your shoulder. Lift your hip and engage through the side of your waist to raise up on the side of your foot or knee. Hold for one minute each side.

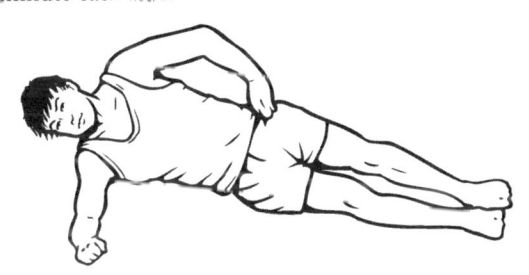

Squats
With feet slightly wider than shoulder width, hands on hips and toes pointing outwards, push your bottom back and down as if to take a seat (you should be able to wriggle your toes). Repeat twenty times.

Step-ups
Anywhere there is a step, step up and down twenty times, then change to lead with the other leg.

Stair climbs
Anywhere there are decent stairs, climb quickly, jog or run up and down four times, rest for thirty seconds, repeat four times.

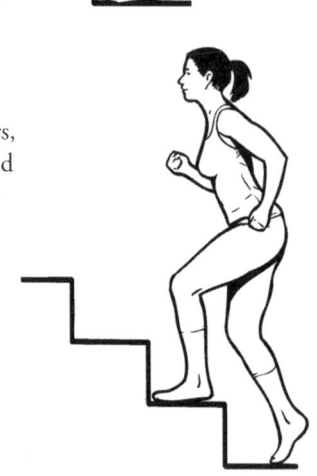

Dips
For these you will need an unmoveable surface around knee height, such as the side of a bath. Place your hands behind you on to the surface, with your bottom in front and off the edge, knees bent. Bending your elbows, dip your bottom towards to the floor, then straighten your elbows to return to the starting position. Repeat twelve to fifteen times.

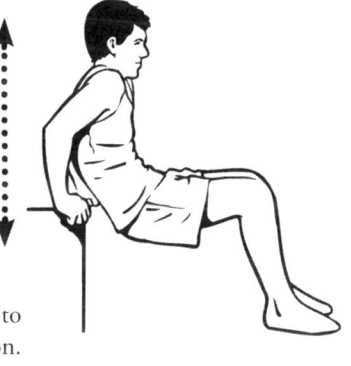

> **WEB SEARCH**
> For more exercises and fitness-related gear see
> www.travelfitness.com, www.acefitness.org or
> www.topendsports.com

10

JOURNEY'S END

A man travels the world in search of what he needs and returns home to find it.

George Moore

- Time to come home
- Sharing experiences
- Keeping the memory alive
- Journeys without end

TIME TO COME HOME

I love Europe: its palpable history, its wealth of culture, its beauty and its people. I love to recognise the threads of my own ancestry and the foundations of customs that Australia has adopted as its own. But I love coming home. Perhaps the pleasure of travelling is intimately connected to the knowledge that there's somewhere to go home to, an anchor in the drifting world, a known place that patiently awaits our return.

After long weeks of travel I relish the comfort of my own bed and the ease (and variety) of my wardrobe. But more, I'm glad to return to the fragrance of eucalypts, the raucous hilarity of the kookaburras in the early morning, the wash of stars across a huge sky: the things that make this uniquely home.

Customs

You know you're back in Australia when you're greeted by a beagle in an official red jacket, sniffing at your luggage and getting excited about your backpack because you used it for market shopping in Greece. Because Australia is an island, the quarantine procedures are more rigorous than at most other destinations. Luggage goes through X-ray screening and quarantine officers open everything. It delays the moment of release into your hometown, but it's a necessary and inescapable step towards freedom.

When you pack for your return flight, put all the items you'll need to declare in an easily accessible place in your suitcase. Just before landing back in Australia, the flight crew will hand out customs declaration forms. Complete the form honestly, and include anything you even think might be suspect.

TRAVEL TIP
- when you fill in your Incoming Passenger Card, err on the safe side and declare anything you think might be suspect
- check Australian Customs' website to know what you can and can't bring back into Australia
- avoid all animal and plant products (even benign-looking potpourri)
- declare if you've been on a farm (the customs officer will clean your shoes for free!)
- always declare food products for checking – packaged foods are usually allowed but don't assume
- declare wildlife souvenirs (check in advance with the Department of Environment and Heritage that you're not buying products from endangered species)
- don't return home with pirated or counterfeit goods

WEB SEARCH
www.customs.gov.au > travellers for quarantine information
www.deh.gov.au/travel to check that wildlife souvenirs have not come from endangered species

Duty-free goods
There are limits to the value and amount of goods purchased overseas and brought back into Australia, including alcoholic beverages and cigarettes, but you can pool your allowance if you're travelling with family. At present, you can bring home A$900 worth of goods (A$450 for under 18 year olds); for those

over 18, you can bring in 2.25 litres of alcoholic beverages, and 250 cigarettes or 250 grams of cigars or tobacco products. For more detailed information, download the Guide for Travellers brochure from the Australian Customs service website: **www.customs.gov.au**

TRAVEL TIP
If you plan to buy electronic equipment duty free:
- know your prices; duty free is not necessarily cheaper
- know your products
- keep in mind that if you have problems with the equipment you may not be able to seek repair or replacement

SHARING EXPERIENCES

The strange thing about returning home after a special holiday is that you usually find nothing has changed. You feel different – expanded by your new knowledge, changed in important ways by your experiences – so it's disorienting to find that the world at home has gone on just the same, barely registering your absence. Pick up a newspaper: nothing's changed. Go to work: people politely ask you about your holidays, then move on to the same concerns that existed before you went away. Your time away, which had seemed so long and vital, contracts into a tiny kernel of a thing and your friends and family fail to recognise what pearls of wisdom you can now impart. We simply have to acknowledge that the experiences are ours alone, embedded now in our very being, and impossible to truly lay out in all their splendour before others.

On the other hand, among those who love to travel, talk of experiences and places often dominates a dinner-party conversation. Swapping anecdotes, smiling over shared experiences, learning about new places, discussing the latest airline deal; these are lively conversations filled with all the exuberance and colour of the world's great cities, with the charm and friendliness of tiny rural villages.

Talk turns to world politics and there's perhaps a greater tolerance and understanding of some of the world's dire problems.

It turns to climate change, and there's a greater appreciation of the urgency, having seen extreme examples of the effect of change in the Northern Hemisphere.

KEEPING THE MEMORY ALIVE

For this dinner party, the table is set with placemats from Vienna, candles from Portugal, a pottery bowl from Spain. The music is French; the food ranges from Italian to Turkish. (The wine is Australian!)

While we may return with tangible souvenirs, more importantly, if we've been alert to the cultures we've travelled through, we can bring home new and colourful customs to integrate into our normal everyday life. Food is probably the most obvious part of our life that is influenced and made richer by our experiences; anyone who has travelled through Europe comes home with a heightened appreciation of good bread.

But there are many other habits you might adopt. I love the way northern Europeans hang out their carpets and doonas to absorb sunshine; how the French wash in a tub placed inside the sink (great for saving water for the pot plants); the brilliant way German women wear scarves; the Italian love affair with *bella figura*; the use of bicycles in even the coldest climates; how the Danes wrap themselves in blankets to dine outside; hot chocolate served in white fluted bowls in Norway. Each is a small symbol of a way of life for people in different parts of the world. Each is highly transportable to home, to stitch into your own everyday routines. The result is a more intricately embroidered pattern of life.

Memories of sublime beauty, or extraordinary kindness, of wonderful food, of funny experiences – tuck them all away to recall whenever you need a lift. I have one special memory of Tuscany that sums up much about that lovely region and acts as a hook to other memories. Waiting for a train at a tiny station on a Sunday morning, the air was full of typical Tuscan sounds: church bells and roosters, and the gunshots of the locals out to find the last remaining bird. On a bench opposite sat an elderly man, smoking; above his head was a sign: *Grazie, Non Fumo*.

Reading about the countries you have visited is a good way to remind you of where you've been. It's deeply satisfying to read about foreign places that you know. You might also read to fill in the gaps of your knowledge about the places you've been. Such reading helps you to understand more deeply what you have seen and is part of the process of whetting the appetite for future travels.

Watch movies that will recall the beauty you've been privileged to see: *Il Postino*, *Stealing Beauty*, *Going West*, *Three Colours Blue*. There are so many great films that capture the essence of a place and its people.

If we learn to see more clearly while we are travelling, because of the strangeness and the time to indulge in careful observation, we can return with fresh eyes to better see what's around us at home. By keeping alive your heightened perception you will find that a trip on a suburban train in Melbourne can be as full of colour and character as that on the Paris Metro. Every day holds the promise of something to be observed, to be learnt, to be changed by. You might even learn to be a tourist in your own town.

Over time, your sharpened perceptions become dulled by routine. This is a sign that it's time to start planning the next trip.

A few of my favourite things

Beside me on my desk is a cobblestone from the streets of Lisbon – a hefty dark grey cube that recalls cobbled streets patterned in light and dark stone. It's a talisman of previous travels, a symbol of another world and another time. A small tangible reminder of a special experience, it's now a paperweight.

Souvenirs do have a place, of course, but rather than the obvious, think about finding small things that you'll use every day, so that they routinely remind you of your travels. I have a potato peeler (how basic is that?) purchased at lovely Balleymaloe House in Ireland. It reminds me of a walk along the banks of the stream that flows through that property, with long grasses bending to the rush of water, and white drifts of snowdrops like sheets spread out to dry beneath the oak trees. Oh, and the glorious food . . .

Memories are lighter than feathers, so you can bring home thousands. Choose your souvenirs to be triggers for those memories: a CD by artists you saw perform, a printed menu that a restaurant was happy for you to take away, a postcard of an artwork from an exhibition you visited.

Bookmarks are good, so light in your case and something to complement the pleasure of reading. A calendar with images of a place you've visited will give you a stab of delight every time you turn the page to a new month – a lovely way to eke out the memories.

Table linen is lovely, crisp white linen from Ireland especially. And small items for the table: pottery dishes, candlesticks, a pepper grinder or delicate espresso cups are just some things to consider.

Fred once bought beautiful handkerchiefs in Rome, which still have the power to transform the dreariness of ironing. Years ago, also in Rome, we purchased a Pavoni espresso machine and for all its temperamental inefficiencies, it was a sculptural piece with its long pressure arm and gleaming chrome, and a true symbol of that city.

Everyday clothes don't cut it as souvenirs (or maybe Italian shoes do). They can be very weighty, but more than this, it's quite difficult to find something truly different from what you can buy at home. But small accessories are worthwhile, such as leather gloves, a silk tie, a belt, or a beautiful shawl. It goes without saying to ignore all the kitsch, such as snowflake jumpers from Norway, or clogs from Holland.

Sporting items, such as skiing or sailing gear, can be good buys overseas if you know the price you'd normally pay at home, but they can be bulky.

TRAVEL TIP
- keep in mind Australian quarantine regulations when buying souvenirs
- if you've been clever enough to pack old clothes that you don't mind leaving behind, you'll have more space for your special purchases
- consider mailing home (surface mail) some items – but check postal costs first

- if you're posting books or brochures, check to see if there is a cheaper 'printed papers' postal rate
- pack fragile items in the your hand luggage, or in the centre of your case wedged in tightly with soft clothing

Photos

Most people come home with hundreds of photographs, which either stay in the camera or on the laptop, never to be sorted, rarely looked at. Make some time when you return home to go through and select your favourite images, and have them printed so they are easily accessible for you to moon over, or to show friends and family.

JOURNEYS WITHOUT END

It's the first cold day for the year, and I pull on a jacket I haven't worn since Prague last year. In the pocket is the butt of a ticket to a concert at the Smetana Hall. I am immediately transported back to one of the most memorable cultural evenings of my life. The concert hall is within the Municipal House, a magnificent Art Nouveau building resplendent with gold trimmings, stained-glass windows and early twentieth-century artwork. Mucha's evocative curving patterns are repeated throughout the building.

It was a bitterly cold evening when we emerged from the concert hall, our heads spinning from a performance of Beethoven's Ninth Symphony with the full Czech Philharmonic Orchestra and both the Czech and Prague choirs. The music was ravishing, almost spiritual. It was a passport into the classical world that is at the heart of European history and culture, there in that golden setting we shared the experience with locals recently emerged from political oppression, who accept such performances as their birthright.

Such are holiday memories: precious moments of enchantment that stay with you forever; that spur you on to further travels.

READING GUIDE

John Armstrong, *The Secret Power of Beauty*
Jane Austen
Honoré de Balzac, *Père Goriot*
John Banville, *Prague Pictures*
Louis de Bernières, *Captain Corelli's Mandolin*
Heinrich Böll, *Irish Diary*
Alain de Botton, *The Art of Travel*
Malcolm Bradbury, *To the Hermitage*
Gerald Brenan, *The Face of Spain*
Mikhail Bulgakov, *The Master and Margarita*
Larry Buttrose, *The Maze of the Muse*
Susan Cahill (ed.), *Desiring Italy*
Tracy Chevalier, *Girl with a Pearl Earring*
Charmian Clift, *Mermaid Singing*
Phil Cousineau, *The Art of Pilgrimage*
Robert Dessaix, *Corfu*
Robert Dessaix, *Do You Speak English?*
Giuseppe di Lampedusa, *The Leopard*
Charles Dickens
Lawrence Durell, *The Alexandria Quartet*
Lawrence Durell, *Prospero's Cell*
Beverley Farmer, *The House in the Light*
Patrick Leigh Fermor, *A Time of Gifts*
Michael Frayn, *Headlong*
Anna Funder, *Stasiland*
Günter Grass, *The Tin Drum*
Robert Graves, *I Claudius* and *Claudius the God*
Nathaniel Hawthorne, *The Marble Faun*
Ernest Hemingway, *For Whom The Bell Tolls*
Peter Hoeg, *Miss Smilla's Feeling for Snow*
Alistaire Horne, *Le Belle France*

Donald Horne, *The Intelligent Tourist*
Henry James, *The Wings of the Dove*
Christopher Koch, *The Many-Coloured Land*
Milan Kundera
Andrea Levy, *Small Island*
Barzini Luigi, *Italians*
Fitzroy MacLean, *Eastern Approaches*
Geert Mak's, *In Europe*
Andrei Makine
Hilary Mantel, *A Place of Greater Safety*
Robert Massie, *Peter the Great*
John Julius Norwich, *A History of Venice*
Orhan Pamuk, *Istanbul: Memories of a City*
John Prebble, *The Highland Clearances*
Peter Robb, *Midnight in Sicily*
Geoffrey Robertson, *The Tyrannicide Brief*
Joseph Roth, *The Radetsky March*
José Saramago, *Journey to Portugal*
SBS, *World Guide*
Colin Thurbron, *To Siberia*
Leo Tolstoy
Sigrid Undset, *Kristen Lavransdatter*
Jane Urquart, *Away*
Rebecca West, *Black Lamb and Grey Falcon*
Virginia Woolf, *Mrs Dalloway*

More Great Books from The Five Mile Press

JOURNEYS

Modern Australian Short Stories

Edited by Barry Oakley

This collection of acclaimed short stories is the perfect reading material for any trip.

Every one of these compelling narratives focuses upon a human journey through either the physical or psychological world. Barry Oakley has chosen these brilliant stories not only for their considerable entertainment value, but for the insight they offer into all of our lives.

Featuring top stories by Cate Kennedy, Tim Winton, Helen Garner, David Malouf, Steve J. Spears and Margo Lanagan, as well as many more of Australia's best contemporary writers, this is the perfect book to slip into your suitcase. It also makes a perfect gift for those overseas friends.

ISBN: 978 1 74178 457 2

More Great Books from The Five Mile Press

LOVE & DESIRE

Four Modern Australian Novellas

Edited by Cate Kennedy

Sometimes, especially on a long-distance plane trip, you need reading material that is longer than a short story, but not as long as a novel. This collection of novellas will do the trick perfectly.

Love & Desire showcases the power and range of the novella form in four exciting new voices.

Paddy O'Reilly in *Deep Water* offers us scenes from an inner life that is tenaciously trying to cling to the familiar as her large family implodes around her.

In Christopher Currie's *Dearly Departed* we spend a humid evening in a Queensland garden with a broken-hearted Lenard Wenn as he grapples with lost love.

Ellen Rodger in *The Girls' Room* has produced a vividly splendid novella as she contrasts the grinding reality of work in the massage parlour with images of a more hopeful relationship developing elsewhere.

The fourth novella, *China* by Margaret Innes, won the inaugural *Meanjin*/Readings novella competition. A poised and elegant work, it describes a woman coming to terms with her real self.

ISBN: 978 1 74178 355 1